Nothing Is Sacred

Nothing Is Sacred

Economic Ideas for the New Millennium

Robert J. Barro

The MIT Press
Cambridge, Massachusetts
London, England

First MIT Press paperback edition, 2003

This book was set in Palatino by Achorn Graphic Services Inc. in QuarkXPress and was printed and bound in the United States of America.

Library of Congress Cataloging-in-Publication Data

Barro, Robert J.
    Nothing is sacred: economic ideas for the new millennium/Robert J. Barro.
        p. cm.
    Includes bibliographical references and index.
    ISBN 0-262-02526-4 (hc.: alk. paper), 0-262-52415-5 (pb)
        1. Economics—History—20th century. 2. Economists—History—20th century. 3. United States—Economic policy—1993–2001.
    4. United States—Economic policy—2001– I. Title.

HB87 .B293 2002
330—dc21

2002024435

10 9 8 7 6 5 4 3 2

For Rachel, to whom I owe the title of this book and many other things

Contents

Introduction

People often ask me why I became an economist. In college and before that, I tended toward mathematics and science. As a physics major at Caltech in the early 1960s, I was lucky to take the two-year sequence taught to freshmen and sophomores the one and only time by the great Richard Feynman. (To prove this, I have a signed and leather-bound copy of the notes from his course.) Feynman's approach was to skip the standard topics in physics and deal instead with frontier material. That was partly why many of the faculty and graduate students attended the course. It also meant that I learned early on what it would mean to be an actual physicist, and I decided pretty quickly that I would not be a great one. In retrospect, it was fortunate that I learned this so soon, rather than having to wait until my senior year or, perhaps, even to graduate school.

I had some exposure to economics from my brother, Steve, who was studying the subject in the 1960s in graduate school. This exposure motivated me to take my first course in economics as a junior at Caltech. Since Steve gets considerable teasing from his leftist friends about his right-wing brother, he may possibly regret this long-ago influence.

I find it amazing now that my first economics class, taught by Alan Sweezy, used John Maynard Keynes's *General Theory of Income and Employment* as the textbook. Although this book is one of the most influential works of the twentieth century, it makes a really lousy textbook. Moreover, since I now regard Keynes's analysis as seriously flawed, it is surprising that I enjoyed the course so much. As a student, I appreciated the simple way that the Keynesian model explained the workings and failings of the overall economy. Especially appealing were the clever policy remedies, such as increased government spending and tax cuts, that Keynes recommended to combat unemployment. Too bad that I discovered later that the model was theoretically and empirically deficient!

Bolstered by the Keynesian inspiration from my junior year course, I decided to make economics my career (although Caltech's rules at the time did not permit a major in economics). This switch in fields turned out to be one of the best decisions I have ever made. I also remember my time as an undergraduate at Caltech as the most academically challenging of my life. This description accords with Caltech's recognition as one of the nation's top undergraduate colleges. However, I have been greatly disappointed that Caltech never followed

MIT's lead by seeking to become as first rate in economics as it is in the "hard sciences."

I was attracted initially to economics because of its application of analytical methods to macroeconomic issues and policies. In fact, the emphasis on mathematics in economic research made it easy for me to make the transition from my undergraduate training in physics. My later periods as an economics Ph.D. student at Harvard and as a faculty member at various universities have been easy in comparison to my undergraduate experience. Perhaps I just had a greater aptitude for economics than for physics, because I do not believe that economics is intrinsically an easier subject.

I learned later that economic reasoning was not just mathematics and could be applied to a wide variety of social problems. Now, I think that no forms of social interaction—including religion, love, crime, and fertility choice—are immune from the power of economic reasoning. Hence, even widely held beliefs—for example, that beauty is an illegitimate credential of a worker or that democracy is important for economic growth—are not sacred truths and are subject to analysis. That is why the title of this book is *Nothing Is Sacred*. Intellectual pursuit in a free society such as ours is about reasoning and not about reaching forgone conclusions—at least not if one wants to obtain new economic ideas for the new millennium.

Early on in my career—at least through graduate school in economics at Harvard and into my stint as an assistant professor at Brown in the early 1970s—I was a standard twentieth-century liberal. Thus, my main approach to economic problems was to design clever government policies that could help to fix things.

Later, particularly influenced by my first experience at the University of Chicago from 1972 to 1975, I became more impressed by the efficiency of private markets and less enamored with the curative role of government. I would describe my underlying philosophy since that time as libertarian or classical liberal rather than conservative or Republican. As I said in the introduction to my book *Getting It Right*, "My views are more akin to the nineteenth-century liberal philosophy espoused by Milton Friedman, especially in his *Capitalism and Freedom*. In that work, he proposed many policies that are harmonious with free markets and are receiving serious attention in the United States and other countries. This list includes school choice, the flat-rate income tax, rules for monetary stability, privatized social security, and the elimination of affirmative-action programs."[1]

I also said in *Getting It Right*, "My view is not anarchic; I believe that government has some key functions, notably to define and protect property rights. This heading encompasses national and domestic security and the enactment and enforcement of a system of laws and contracts. . . . My belief in the appropriateness of this limited

1. Robert Barro, *Getting It Right* (Cambridge, Mass.: MIT Press, 1996), p. xiv.

range of public functions is consistent with the view that most governments have gone much too far in their expenditures, taxation, and regulations."

Larry Summers, my colleague at Harvard until 1991 (and later U.S. Treasury secretary and now president of Harvard and sort of my boss), had a view on my philosophy. He told me: "If I had your views on economics, I would find another profession." The point is, for Larry still (and for me when I was a student and junior professor), the main attraction of economics is its scope for designing policies that can improve private choices. If I was right that private markets usually function better without the government's intervention, then Larry thought that economics would be a pretty dull field. Thus, he would find something else to do. Naturally, I have to disagree, because I have found plenty of interesting things to analyze with economic tools even while maintaining my basic free-market approach. Some of this analysis even has interesting implications for government policy.

I have continued to focus my academic research on macroeconomics, perhaps because I started that way, going back to my first undergraduate course. However, I have used my writings in popular media—starting as a contributing editor of *The Wall Street Journal* in 1991 and continuing as a viewpoint columnist with *Business Week* since 1998—to explore the applications of economics more broadly. Many of these topics are discussed in this book.

I begin the book with biographical sketches of some noteworthy persons, mostly economists, whom I have known or read about. I discuss my former colleagues and leaders of the Chicago School of Economics, Milton Friedman, George Stigler, and Gary Becker. I learned a lot from them about the roles of markets and incentives, the wide applicability of economic reasoning, and the close interplay between economics and politics. Some of this work, notably Becker's, has been described as economic imperialism, but I think it is an excellent form of imperialism.

I include comments about the great classical precursors of the Chicago school, Adam Smith and David Ricardo. Smith is noted for extolling and explaining the virtues of markets and individual incentives. Ricardo is known for constructing a coherent macroeconomic framework, which can be used to study economic growth, taxes, public debt, and other matters.

I talk about Robert Mundell, who essentially invented international macroeconomics during a remarkably productive spurt at Chicago and the International Monetary Fund in the 1960s. I discuss Bob Lucas, a more recent pillar of Chicago, who taught me the implications of rational expectations for macroeconomic and other models.

I include a few thoughts about my Harvard colleague John Kenneth Galbraith, who was the hero of my leftist youth. Unfortunately, he later inspired me indirectly by convincing me that his big-government views were misguided. I also have thoughts on Larry Summers, whom I have already mentioned. Later I discuss Domingo Cavallo, who was a great hero for Argentina in 1991 but who failed in his second coming in 2001.

More surprisingly, I have a childhood remembrance of Joe DiMaggio and some commentary on Bono, the well-known rock star, amateur economist, and advocate for global justice. I also include in this section some remarks about Al Gore on environmental philosophy and George W. Bush on compassionate conservatism. No doubt these two political figures do not measure up intellectually to the others in this section (with the possible exception of DiMaggio but surely not Bono). But I guess politicians deserve some attention.

In a section on social issues, I consider the applications of economic thinking to some interesting social issues. I begin with a discussion of the economics of beauty. My politically incorrect position is that physical attractiveness and intelligence are essentially parallel as characteristics that are valued in the labor market (or elsewhere). Then I discuss a controversial study that links the expansion of abortion rights in the United States in the early 1970s to the reductions in crime that occurred a couple of decades later.

I also assess U.S. drug control policy in the context of policies toward Colombia, a country that has been driven apart by the drug problem. My central argument favors a movement toward legalization of drugs. When I wrote a column on this topic for *Business Week*, I expected wide attention—indeed, this column inspired more e-mails than any other I have written. However, I was surprised by the favorable tone of most of the readers.

I next investigate the popular argument that college admissions tests, including the SATs, have little predictive value for college grades. My findings are that these scores have substantial, though imperfect, predictive content, and not just for the freshman year.

I assess arguments for sustaining intellectual property rights through copyrights and patents by considering the cases of Napster and Prozac. The issues are not straightforward, but I am particularly concerned that abridgments of rights will sharply curtail the supply of new music, new pharmaceuticals, and other innovations.

I also look at the famous Microsoft antitrust case. My concern here is that U.S. antitrust policy tends to penalize success and innovation and has doubtful benefits for consumers.

Finally, I look at personal accounts for social security. I criticize the free-lunch arguments that have been offered about rates of return, but I nevertheless favor personal accounts because of their expansions of property rights and personal choice.

My recent work on macroeconomics has stressed long-term issues, including the determinants of long-run economic growth. From the standpoint of fighting world poverty, nothing is more important than figuring out which policies differentiate the fast-growing countries from the slow-growing ones. In this spirit, I focus the third section of the book on economic growth.

I first look at the regions of the former East and West Germany to understand issues of economic convergence. Particularly important in this case is the adverse consequence of the west's treating the east as a welfare client. I then look at the recent growth experiences in East Asia, stressing the role of the Asian financial crisis. I argue that the West may help by owning parts of the financial system and by providing the basis for widespread use of a strong foreign currency, such as the U.S. dollar. This monetary setup is often termed *dollarization*, although it can involve the use of the euro or another money rather than the dollar. However, I found that such suggestions led to charges of Yankee imperialism.

Next, I consider the interplay between inequality and growth and argue that the interactions are weak. Thus, I question the argument that equalization of incomes tends to foster better economic performance.

Other essays consider aspects of democracy or its absence, as observed in the new Congo, Chile, and Mexico. Throughout this discussion, I question the romantic focus of U.S. foreign policy on promoting democracy in all times and places. My cross-country research has convinced me that the rule of law and property rights are more important than democracy in the promotion of economic growth. Moreover, democracy—measured, say, by indexes of political rights or civil liberties—is not the same as the rule of law.

I look next at currency boards and currency unions. First, I discuss my Twilight Zone–like trip in August 1998 to Russia, where I unsuccessfully proposed the introduction of a currency board. Then I consider Ecuador's recent move to full use of the U.S. dollar. Finally, I discuss my experience with Davos's famous World Economic Forum, and I offer my views on the future of the International Monetary Fund.

The last section of the book deals with fiscal and monetary policies and other macroeconomic topics, primarily in a U.S. context. I discuss issues of U.S. budgets and tax cuts, and I relate the tendency of institutions to spend free cash, first, to the U.S. Congress and, later, to the American Economic Association. I also assess the likely economic consequences of the September 11 attacks and the resulting war on terrorism. Then I consider some general insights on budget policies that can be obtained from an international study of fiscal reforms.

Next, I carry out a quantitative evaluation of all the completed U.S. presidential administrations since Truman's second term. This evaluation is based on contributions to economic growth, unemployment, inflation, and interest rates. The best outcomes are for Reagan's first term and Clinton's second term. Of course, this sort of analysis does not isolate the effect of the president, and, in particular, it fails to distinguish luck from conscious policy.

I look at Chairman Alan Greenspan's tenure as chairman of the Federal Reserve, and I make an irreverent comparison between him and Chance the Gardener (the Peter Sellers character from the movie *Being There*). I am pleased that I feel I have finally achieved some understanding of how the Fed actually conducts monetary policy, but I am concerned that the policy became overly expansionary in 2001.

Another essay considers attempts by economists and political scientists to predict the outcomes of presidential elections, such as the one in 2000. Economic factors have substantial predictive content, but they did poorly in predicting outcomes during the 1990s. However, this analysis did well in predicting nearly a dead heat for the 2000 race.

The penultimate essay discusses oil and complains about the tendency of U.S. public officials to treat as friends countries that attempt to hold back supplies of oil. The final essay assesses the U.S. stock market and concludes that efficient-markets approaches are superior to analyses that purport to find irrationalities in one direction or the other.

This book covers a wide territory, and the unifying theme is less in the topics than in the underlying approach. Hence, my method for applying basic economic principles is similar whether I am studying standard economic problems, such as economic growth and monetary policy, or nonstandard ones, such as democracy, beauty, and abortion rights. The main thing I can promise readers is that I am trying to assess important questions in a logical and interesting way. It is not my fault if readers get upset by some of the logical conclusions.

1

Thoughts on Friends
and Other
Noteworthy Persons

Milton Friedman and His Memoirs

At the Harvard University that I knew as a graduate student in the late 1960s, Milton Friedman was treated as a right-wing midwestern crank. Most of the derision applied to his views on money, including the argument that inflation was always and everywhere a monetary phenomenon. However, even the permanent-income theory of consumption—his scientifically impeccable model in which consumer demand depended on a household's anticipated long-run income—was subjected to poorly reasoned criticism.

Friedman's contributions to public policy, as expressed most effectively in *Capitalism and Freedom*, were dismissed by being ignored.[1] Thus, we unfortunate Ph.D. students did not learn about his prescient ideas on school vouchers, the flat-rate income tax, the all-volunteer army,

---

1. Milton Friedman, *Capitalism and Freedom* (Chicago: University of Chicago Press, 1962).

welfare reform through a negative income tax, privatized social security, flexible exchange rates, and rules for money growth and balanced budgets. Many of these once-radical ideas that Milton had advanced by the 1950s have become mainstream policies, and others are on the active agenda. The all-volunteer army has worked well for many years, the earned-income tax credit is a form of negative income tax, the flat-rate income tax is likely to be a serious proposal in future Congresses, and school vouchers are under consideration in many states and in Washington, D.C. The current debate on U.S. social security reform is primarily over the extent and form of private accounts rather than the wisdom of any privatization. Some years from now, we may experience a similar debate about the details of drug legalization, one of Friedman's more recent policy proposals and a topic that I consider in the next section of this book.

Milton's winning of a Nobel Prize in 1976 was only one indication that the economics profession had accepted the importance of his contributions. In fact, the only person to rival Friedman for policy influence in the twentieth century is John Maynard Keynes, who had a strikingly different view of the role of government. Keynes was influential because he advocated more government intervention into what he perceived as poorly functioning private economies caught up in the Great Depression. In contrast to Keynes, Friedman put the main blame for the Depression on government failures, especially of monetary policy. Hence, the Depression did not make Friedman a fan of big government. He also found in the Federal Reserve's failure to prevent deflation an argument in favor of monetary rules. As the world evolved— with low inflation becoming the major mission of central banks and free markets and secure property rights becoming the main policies to promote economic growth—Friedman surely won the intellectual battle.

Noneconomists who want to know about Friedman's ideas are best advised to read *Capitalism and Freedom* and *Free to Choose*. But his autobiography (*Two Lucky People*, written with his wife, Rose, and published by the University of Chicago Press) fills in many of the facts about his transition from pariah to priest.[2] For me, a key lesson is that Friedman's influence was achieved mainly through the force of ideas, not by direct participation in the policy process. Except for work during World War II, including an unfortunate contribution to the establishment of income tax withholding, he avoided government employment. Thus, the key advice to academic economists in his memoirs is, "By all means spend a few years in Washington—but only a few. If you stay more than two or three you will become addicted and will be unable effectively to return to a scholarly career."[3] My only

---

2. Milton Friedman and Rose Friedman, *Free to Choose* (Orlando: Harcourt Brace, 1979); Milton Friedman and Rose Friedman, *Two Lucky People, Memoirs* (Chicago: University of Chicago Press, 1998).
3. Friedman and Friedman, *Two Lucky People*, p. 110.

disagreement is that two or three years in Washington are too many to retain one's scientific edge.

In a similar vein with regard to congressional testimony, Friedman says, "I long ago decided it was a waste of time to testify before congressional committees. . . . Spending the same time writing an op-ed piece . . . or giving a talk is a more efficient use of time for the purpose of influencing policy."[4] (I was pleased as a regular contributor to *Business Week* to learn that writing op-ed pieces is an okay use of one's time.) Friedman particularly had great influence in writing for *Newsweek* from 1966 to 1984, although his termination in favor of a couple of mere reporters was perhaps not the most brilliant decision in the history of journalism.

My biggest complaint about Friedman's memoirs is the omission of the best photograph of him that I know of. This picture, taken by George Stigler, the codeveloper of the Chicago school of economics, shows Friedman receiving a speeding ticket from a policeman on Lake Shore Drive in Chicago. Although he apparently found it optimal to break the law, the picture shows clearly that he was cooperating fully with the local authorities.

Milton, along with Friedrich von Hayek, was one of the founders of the Mont Pelerin Society, an important international association of libertarians. When I was a junior colleague of Milton at the University of Chicago in

---

4. Ibid., p. 363.

1974, I was invited to present a paper at the upcoming Mont Pelerin meetings in Hong Kong. Naturally, I consulted with Milton about whether I should attend. Surprisingly, he replied that the society ought to be abolished. He explained that the organization had served an important function after World War II by providing a means for libertarians in many small countries to interact with like-minded persons in the United States and other larger countries. But he felt that by 1974, many outlets existed for libertarian discussions, so that the society was no longer needed. Moreover, he argued that institutions tended to become self-perpetuating and never went out of business, even when their purpose had been served. He thought that the Mont Pelerin Society ought to set an example by declaring victory and going out of business.

Unfortunately, I took Milton's argument as advice not to attend the meeting in Hong Kong, and I declined the invitation. By doing so, I missed out on many useful years of interaction with interesting thinkers who participated in the Mont Pelerin conferences. It was not until 1992 that I first attended a meeting of the society.

We are fortunate that Friedman had the good humor and self-confidence to persevere in the face of many years of scorn by left-wing economists and journalists. The tables were turned on his detractors many years ago and—to borrow from his famous quote about Keynes—we are all Friedmanians now.

Adam Smith, Including Thoughts on Ken Galbraith and David Ricardo

In April 1997, I joined my Harvard colleague Ken Galbraith and other economists for a symposium at the University of Pennsylvania on the contributions of Adam Smith. I began my remarks with a recollection of my first encounter with Ken.

In the mid-1960s, I was a typical left-wing undergraduate student at Caltech. For any social problem that arose, I had no doubt that the appropriate cure involved some form of government intervention. So, naturally, Galbraith was my hero, and I was therefore greatly excited when he came to my school in 1964 to give a speech in support of Lyndon Johnson's campaign for the presidency. I confess that I cannot remember a lot of the details of the speech, but I know that I was disappointed. In particular, I recall feeling that his arguments for bigger government were not compelling. No doubt, this event started me on the road to doubting the wisdom of governmental activism and appreciating the wonders of free markets.

When I discussed this experience with Ken after more than thirty years, his surprising reaction was to apologize for what must have been a bad speech. He said that he especially regretted his endorsement of Lyndon Johnson, who was later to become anathema to liberals because of his pursuit of the Vietnam War. If it had been me, I would have apologized mainly for Johnson's Great

Society programs. But, anyhow, during the panel debate in Pennsylvania, I made the rash prediction that if the 1964 presidential election were rerun, Ken and I would both vote for the great conservative, Barry Goldwater. Galbraith vigorously disagreed with this contention, and the audience applauded his position.

The time from the 1960s through the early 1970s can now be seen as a peak in the influence of left-wing thought in U.S. policy. From Johnson, we had such social welfare programs as Medicare, Medicaid, public housing, food stamps, and aid for education. From Nixon, we got the Occupational Safety and Health Administration (OSHA), the Environmental Protection Agency (EPA), the Endangered Species Act, and a major expansion of social security benefits. We also got price controls and the 55 mile-per-hour speed limit. Given all this unfortunate activism, I think that Nixon certainly deserved to be impeached, though for economic policy rather than Watergate.

In the macroeconomic area, the accepted wisdom was that good things could happen only if the government continually intervened to smooth out the business cycle and to stimulate long-term economic growth. Central planning and socialism were applauded as ways to promote economic development, for example, in the former colonies of Africa and in the Communist bloc. Although the Soviet Union and the other centrally planned economies were seen as repressive on human rights, they appeared to be functioning well economically and, perhaps, to be poised for an eventual overtaking of the free-enterprise West.

Times have certainly changed. Now the formerly centrally planned economies are viewed as economic disasters that are making difficult transitions to capitalism with a mixed amount of success. There is a consensus that economic prosperity in developing countries requires institutions that foster free markets and sustain property rights and the rule of law. There is also a presumption that private enterprise is more efficient than public ownership; the main hurdle to successful privatization in most countries is the political power of vested interests. Almost no one—not even the leader of Britain's Labour party—believes that government should own and operate the major means of production.

Moreover, the new orthodoxy is based not merely on ideology but on hard data. In the experience of over one hundred countries since 1960, there is evidence that economic growth and investment are strengthened by better maintenance of the rule of law, greater openness to markets domestically and internationally, and smaller levels of nonproductive government expenditures. Also helpful are investments in education and health, low fertility rates, and low inflation. In effect, the world ran the race between free markets and central planning, and free markets—and, hence, Adam Smith—won.

Adam Smith is, of course, justly lauded for his advocacy of free markets and limited government. Particularly famous is his idea that each person's pursuit of self-interest leads, as if by an invisible hand, to socially efficient outcomes: "By directing that industry in such a manner as its produce may be of the greatest value, he intends only his own gain, and he is in this, as in many other cases, led by an invisible hand to promote an end which was no part of his intention. Nor is it always the worse for society that it was no part of it. By promoting his own interest he frequently promotes that of the society more efficiently than when he really intends to promote it. I have never known much good done by those who affected to trade for the public good."[5]

Brilliant insight to be sure, yet disappointing because this proposition, like most others in *The Wealth of Nations*, are more the product of the author's unmatched intuition than they are conclusions from a theory. One does not need mathematics or other formalism to appreciate if then propositions. Smith focuses on the "then" without the "if" or particularly on the connection between the "if" and the "then." This is not to deny that he usually gets the right answer and that *The Wealth of Nations* is one of the all-time great books. But it is hard for ordinary people or even economists to use the book's framework to evaluate policies or go beyond the answers that Smith provides.

Smith also stresses the idea that monopoly leads to excessive prices and to inefficient management. He says,

5. Adam Smith, *The Wealth of Nations*, 6th ed. (London: A. Strahan, 1791, v.II, Book IV, p. 181).

for example, "People of the same trade seldom meet together, even for merriment and diversion, but the conversation ends in a conspiracy against the public, or in some contrivance to raise prices." And, further, "Monopoly . . . is a great enemy to good management, which can never be universally established but in consequence of . . . free and universal competition."[6]

Given all this, one would have expected Smith to advocate antitrust policies to spur free markets. Yet Smith also says, "It is impossible indeed to prevent such meetings [of people in the same trade] by any law which either could be executed, or would be consistent with liberty and justice."[7] This thought accords with much of current thinking by free-market economists about antitrust enforcement—that it tends to do more harm than good. One reason is that the government frequently is captured by the industries that it seeks to regulate. Another reason is that antitrust measures are often a penalty for success, particularly for successful innovations. Finally, antitrust actions are not so valuable because monopoly tends to be temporary except when it has the weight of government behind it.

In contrast to Smith's incomplete modeling, his follower, David Ricardo, provides a coherent setting— basically, the first macroeconomic model—that can be tested, modified, and applied. Although Ricardo is surely narrower and less imaginative and insightful

---

6. Ibid., v. I, Book I, pp. 200, 229.
7. Ibid., p. 200.

than Smith, he is also a lot better organized. That is why Ricardo's analysis of macroeconomics—for example, of the implications of public debt—is more coherent and useful than Smith's. Ricardo, in particular, worked out a famous theorem that proved the equivalence of taxation and public borrowing. That is, under certain conditions, the size of the budget deficit does not matter. Some economists have pointed out that Ricardo did not believe his famous result because he doubted that people behaved in the rational manner postulated by the theorem. Interestingly, however, the theorem is original, but the doubts are pretty much copied from Smith's *Wealth of Nations*. In this case, Smith gets credit for Ricardo's weakness and self-doubt, not for his imagination.

George Stigler, whom I discuss at length in the next essay, was perhaps Adam Smith's greatest fan. George got pretty irritated with me for this sort of criticism of Smith. He particularly got annoyed when I asserted that *The Wealth of Nations* was the greatest collection of one-liners that had ever been assembled. These thoughts were aggravating to George because he liked one-liners so much and because one of his proudest memories was paying only a few hundred dollars at auction for a first edition of *The Wealth of Nations*. (George kept the book in his home in a wooden box on the floor to make it appear valueless to a potential thief.)

Honesty forces me to admit that the market test conflicts with my comparison of Smith and Ricardo. A first edition of *The Wealth of Nations* sold in London a few years ago for upwards of £20,000, whereas a first edition of Ricardo's *Principles of Political Economy and Taxation* fetched a mere £6,500. More puzzling still is that the first edition of Thomas Malthus's *Essay on the Principle of Population*, a work clearly inferior to Smith's or Ricardo's, seemed to be the most expensive economics book, with a price of as much as £30,000. (Of course, one problem with this analysis is that it takes no account of the quantities of each book available.)

Anyway, as is clear from the Adam Smith tie that I wore at the debate with Galbraith, I am obviously a great fan of Smith. Moreover, my purpose was to praise Smith and free markets, not to bury them.

George Stigler and the Chicago School of Economics

In 1982, the U.S. economy was in a recession. George Stigler was awarded the Nobel Prize for economics, and the Reagan administration eagerly invited this kindred spirit to meet the press at the White House. No doubt in order to establish his political independence, George lost no time in describing the ongoing economic downturn as a depression. Then, as he wrote in his *Memoirs of an Unregulated Economist*, he "was removed from the platform in a manner reminiscent of vaudeville days, which is surely appropriate in a theatrical town."[8]

---

8. George Stigler, *Memoirs of an Unregulated Economist*, (New York: Basic Books, 1988) p. 137.

One would like to praise George for his candor, but it was outrageous to argue that 1982, when the unemployment rate peaked at less than 11 percent, was similar to the Great Depression of the early 1930s, when the unemployment rate reached 25 percent. George was right, however, that the 1982 recession was pretty bad.

George's unfortunate news conference in 1982 reminds us that he, like most other great economists, had his main influence on economics and economic policy through research and writings, not as a government policy adviser or by direct communication with the public. (He was offered a position as foreign trade adviser to President Nixon but wisely declined it.) George took seriously John Maynard Keynes's famous dictum (from his *General Theory*) about the subtle influence of economists: "The ideas of economists . . . both when they are right and when they are wrong, are more powerful than is commonly understood. . . . Practical men, who believe themselves to be quite exempt from any intellectual influences, are usually the slaves of some defunct economist. Madmen in authority, who hear voices in the air, are distilling their frenzy from some academic scribbler of a few years back."[9] In the main, George avoided positions in government and allowed his academic scribblings to have an impact on policies and on views about the role of the state in economic affairs. In accord with Keynes's thinking, I have no doubt that Stigler's influence on policy and

9. John Maynard Keynes, *The General Theory of Employment, Interest and Money*, (London: Macmillan, 1936) p. 383.

practical men exceeded that of most economists who spent a lot of time in Washington.

George, along with Milton Friedman, was a principal architect of the Chicago school of economics. George pointed out in his memoirs how he was responsible for Milton's coming to Chicago: "In the spring of 1946 I received the offer of a professorship from the University of Chicago. . . . I went to Chicago, met with the President . . . and I was vetoed! I was too empirical. . . . So the professorship was offered to Milton Friedman, and President Colwell and I had launched the new Chicago School."[10] It was not until 1958 that Stigler returned (in a much more lucrative position as Walgreen Professor) to Chicago, where he had earlier done graduate work with the theorist and social philosopher Frank Knight.

A key tenet of the Chicago school is that free markets function well in most circumstances, so government intervention into the economy ought to be limited. A second theme is that economic analysis has substantial explanatory power for empirical phenomena, not only in the narrow economic realm but also—as Gary Becker (whom I discuss next) has particularly demonstrated—in a wide variety of social interactions.

George's most distinctive contributions to the Chicago school involved studies of the actual effects of government regulations, such as in the electric utility and financial sectors. Although early on, George stressed the evils of monopoly and the hypothetical benefits of antitrust

---

10. Stigler, *Memoirs*, p. 40.

measures—more or less like Adam Smith—he later became convinced that bigness is not necessarily bad and that the consequences of regulation and antitrust enforcement usually depart from the intended effects. The government often ends up hindering competition, promoting inefficiency, and being captured by the industry it is policing.

For George, these typically poor outcomes raised the puzzle of why the government would nevertheless often intervene. He argued that we should examine the relative political influence of the winners and losers to predict what the government would actually do, as opposed to what it ought to do. Thus, tariffs can arise if the protected sectors constitute a concentrated, effective lobby. A similar logic can explain why governmental agencies would often act as protectors of monopoly privileges for the groups they are supposed to regulate. This type of analysis features strong interactions between economics and political science and has had a major impact on the methods that political scientists use.

Stigler received the Nobel Prize for his research in the 1960s on the economics of information. He showed how the dispersion of prices in a market would depend on the costs of search, and he used the framework to explain the roles of advertising, retail stores, and other familiar features of markets. He showed that the maintenance of monopoly pricing was rendered difficult by the costs of observing competitors' prices, and he demonstrated that the government's practice of open bidding meant that it would typically pay high prices. This work on information opened up research areas that are now important in industrial organization, labor economics, and macroeconomics.

Stigler's first and continuing area of research was the history of economic thought. He went beyond mere description of changing economic theories to analyses of how ideas influenced the work of followers and critics. In some cases, he employed data on citations—references to earlier works—to measure objectively the impact of research on subsequent professional practice.

I already mentioned in my essay about Milton Friedman that Milton's discussion had kept me from attending a meeting of the libertarian Mont Pelerin Society, in 1974. It was George who decided later that I ought to participate in the society. He accomplished this end by persuading the board of the society in 1990 that I had already attended two meetings, a prerequisite for membership in the organization. With George's assurance, the board voted me in as a member. Thereby, as far as I know, I became the only nonfounding member of the society who had never previously attended any meetings. (I hope this confession will not result in my ouster.)

George Stigler had a remarkable career, and his ability to continue productive research up to age eighty was likely due to the great variety of his interests. He was also known as a great wit, even to the many victims of his barbs, and his engaging writing style contributed to his wide readership. Thus, it seems fitting to close this discussion with the last piece of his wit that I know about.

George was organizing the general meeting of the Mont Pelerin Society for August 1992 in Vancouver. He had earlier connived to have me voted in as a member. He then invited me to present a paper in Vancouver, but he pointed out that the society would reimburse only the "most economical method of travel." Knowing that George would never fly coach, I accepted the invitation but said that I would "follow your instructions and rely on first-class travel." This weak attempt at humor was squashed by George's reply: "Allow plenty of time in hitchhiking to Vancouver."

George died in December 1991, before the Vancouver meetings. I miss his wit and his economics in roughly equal measure.

Gary Becker, the Great Economic Imperialist

I first met Gary Becker in 1968, when I was a new economics Ph.D. from Harvard. I had managed to arrange a job seminar at Columbia University, where Gary was then employed. At one point during my presentation, a harsh critic arose from the audience and began to attack my work. But before I could respond, Gary took up my cause, went back and forth in argument with my critic, and eventually carried the day.

I thought that this was great. Giving seminars was easy. I could just sit back, and a great economist would come forward and vanquish all of my foes. But, unfortunately, this has never happened to me again.

Gary received the Nobel Prize in 1992, primarily for his applications of economic principles to a wide array of social issues. He began with studies of discrimination in labor markets and showed how persons who wished to discriminate on racial or other grounds tended to bear costs in the marketplace. His other early work, on human capital, showed how investments in education could be treated as analogous to business investments in physical capital. Subsequently, Gary applied economic reasoning to areas such as crime and punishment, marriage, divorce, fertility, addiction, and the formation of preferences.

Some critics view Gary as an economic imperialist, and Gary surely has not been shy about extending the domain of the economic model. But I guess one's opinion of this imperialism depends on one's evaluation of the results. In my view, this broad extension of economics has been helpful for understanding empirical phenomena and designing useful public policies.

It was great when Gary got the Nobel Prize in 1992, an award that was long overdue. David Romer, an economist at Berkeley, had been running a betting pool each year in which people tried to pick the prize winner. Gary was the leader in this pool for each of the five years preceding his award.

One hypothesis about the delay for the award is that the prize committee realizes that recipients tend to shirk once they get the prize. This consideration was particularly important in Gary's case because he had continued to exhibit high productivity. Thus, the drop in output caused by an early prize for Gary might have had severe adverse consequences for economic research. (Actually, this is a pleasant hypothesis that anyone can entertain to explain why he or she has not yet been awarded a Nobel Prize.)

Another point is that sixty-two, Gary's age when he received the prize, is relatively young for economists. The average age of recipients since the prize was first awarded in 1969 is sixty-seven. Interestingly, this average is much higher than those observed in other fields—fifty-nine for chemistry and medicine and fifty-six for physics. Of course, the economics prize is much newer than these others. But it is still surprising that the average age of winners in economics has shown no apparent trend to decline over time. However, the last two awards—in 2000 and 2001—went to younger scholars.

Gary mentioned to me that he did not know how to respond when reporters asked him about his hobbies. For reporters, the application of economic reasoning to areas such as crime, marriage, fertility, and so on could not be considered a hobby. So, finally, Gary said that he came up with tennis as something that he could count as a hobby.

Gary's tennis performance is an example of the pure human capital model. He began with little native talent, then painstakingly built up to a reasonable level of competence after many years of instruction and on-the-job training. The lack of style then became something of a psychological weapon. There was tremendous pressure on opponents not to lose points to someone who seemed to lack athletic flair, and this pressure was often accentuated by Gary's pausing at crucial points and saying things like, "This point is the key. If you can just win this point, then you will probably win the match."

Some years ago, I went to Tucumán, a city in Argentina, to give a series of lectures on economic growth. Tucumán is something of an outpost in the desert for good economics. I met there Professor Cordemí, a Chicago Ph.D. of around 1960, who turned out to be George Stigler's greatest fan. He went on at length about George's brilliance and told me how he applied George's teachings in his own course on the history of economic thought.

Somehow the discussion got around to Gary Becker, and I opined that Gary was also quite a good economist. However, Cordemí began to shake his head in a doleful manner, and I sensed, first, that he did not approve of Becker and, second, that I was losing his respect because of my own good opinion of Becker. Then Cordemí said that Becker's problem was his lack of originality. This was really a surprise—many people object to Gary because he is outrageous, not because he is unoriginal. Then Cordemí dropped his bombshell: all of Becker's ideas are in Philip Wicksteed's book, *The Common Sense of Political Economy*.[11]

---

11. Philip H. Wicksteed, *The Common Sense of Political Economy* (London: Routledge, 1946).

After this revelation, I was pretty eager to get home to consult my copy of *The Common Sense,* which I owned but had not studied. When I read the book, I discovered quickly what Cordemí was referring to. Wicksteed urged his fellow economists to apply economics broadly to a variety of social interactions, not just to usual business matters. However, as far as I could tell, he had not gone anywhere with this idea. Therefore, Gary's originality seemed to be intact. Nevertheless, I filed away this incident and figured I could use it against Gary at some future time.

The moment came when my wife and I were scheduled to play Gary and his brother in a tennis match. Gary had been especially irritating in advance with claims that his team would be victorious. He even pointed out that his brother and he had beaten a pair to whom my wife and I had lost, so that transitivity guaranteed their success. Therefore, I figured that I needed to create something of a psychological edge, and I arranged for my younger son, Josh (then eight years old), to be on the tennis court prior to the big match. He was set up to be reading the *Common Sense of Political Economy.* I figured that Gary would ask Josh what he was reading, and I told Josh to report the author and title and then say, "I understand that you got all your ideas from this fellow." That moment would, I figured, be a good time to start the tennis match.

So Gary walks on the court, goes over to Josh, and says, "Hi, Josh, what are you reading?" Josh duly reported, "*The Common Sense of Political Economy* by Philip Henry Wicksteed," but before he could say any more, Gary quickly responded, "Oh, yes, I copied all his work." Needless to say, Josh was enormously pleased by this confession, which he had thought would take considerable effort to elicit. We then went on to play the big grudge tennis match. I forget how it turned out.

Robert Mundell, the Father of International Macroeconomics

The 1999 winner of the Nobel Prize in economics, Robert Mundell of Columbia University, pretty much invented international macroeconomics with his outpouring of research in the early 1960s. The work took place primarily at the International Monetary Fund (IMF) and the economics department of the University of Chicago. Aside from the research, an important legacy of Mundell's Chicago period was the production of much of the next generation of influential economists in international macroeconomics. His students included Rudi Dornbusch of MIT (whose menial task in the late 1960s included the preparation of the bibliography for the book *International Economics*[12]); Jacob Frenkel, former governor of the Bank of Israel; and Michael Mussa, the recently departed head of research of the IMF.

---

12. Robert a. Mundell, *International Economics* (New York: Macmillan, 1968).

Mundell's principal work is collected in *International Economics*, published in 1968 and curiously out of print for many years. (My recollection is that Mundell had a dispute with the publisher and retrieved the publishing rights many years ago, but no reprinting of this major book has yet occurred.) The research provided a basic framework for analyzing macroeconomic outcomes under fixed or flexible exchange rates.

In the fixed-rate case, monetary policy was constrained by international forces. As is now well known, any attempt by the monetary authority to follow an independent policy would create balance-of-payments problems and eventual changes in the exchange rate. In contrast, monetary policy could be freely chosen under a flexible-rate system.

Mundell's models allowed a significant role for fiscal policy, especially under fixed exchange rates. However, the treatment was entirely Keynesian—an increased budget deficit operated solely by raising the aggregate demand for goods. Moreover, increases in government spending and cuts in taxes had pretty much the same effect on the economy. It was only later, in more popular writings, that Mundell began to emphasize the supply-side, incentive effects from tax rates. Thus, whatever the merits of supply-side economics and Reaganomics—and I would say there are many—these ideas had nothing to do with the work that resulted in a Nobel Prize.

Mundell's 1968 book also contained an important study of optimum currency areas. This work compared the net benefits of a common currency—an extreme form of a fixed exchange rate—with those of a flexible rate. More precisely, Mundell analyzed the desirable size of an economic zone within which transactions would use a single form of money. Nowadays, the term *common currency* is sometimes replaced by *dollarization*, because the dollar is often the preferred money for another country to adopt. However, there are also examples of uses of other foreign moneys, including the German mark and the euro.

The main benefit from a flexible exchange rate was its allowance for an independent monetary policy, which could offset economic disturbances that affected the region in which the money was used. This benefit was significant when regions were hit by different economic shocks and when labor could not move readily across regions. (Later treatments also considered the mobility of capital, technology, and final products.) The principal gain from a common currency was that it facilitated transactions and made price calculations easier. After all, money, like language, would not be useful if everyone used his or her own personal type. The trade-off between these two forces determined the optimal size of a currency zone and, hence, the number of zones that ought to exist in the world.

Economists still use this basic approach to assess alternative currency arrangements. However, modern analyses recognize that independent monetary policies under flexible exchange rates entail a lack of external discipline and may lead to high and volatile inflation. In contrast, the fixing of the exchange rate can commit a country to the inflation rate of the anchor country. This arrangement works well if the anchor currency—such as the U.S. dollar or, in Mundell's vision, something that restores a serious role for gold—behaves properly.

An important caveat is that the announcement of a fixed exchange rate is not enough to ensure commitment, as was demonstrated by the devaluations of several countries in the 1990s. These problems began with Mexico in 1994, then appeared later in several East Asian countries, Russia, Brazil, Turkey, and Argentina. To be successful, a fixed-rate setup has to represent a firm commitment, such as a common-currency setup, which includes the euro zone and actual and proposed dollarizations in Latin America. A currency board, as used by Argentina from 1991 to 2001, appeared to be successful but eventually failed.

I first met Mundell in the late 1960s when he gave a seminar at Harvard where I was a Ph.D. student. After his presentation, we discussed my research on extreme inflation, and he encouraged me to pursue this work and to submit a paper eventually to the *Journal of Political Economy (JPE)*, which he was then editing at the University of Chicago. These words were valuable to me because inflation and money were unpopular research topics at Harvard in the 1960s. Fortunately, I followed Mundell's advice, and my article in the *JPE* in 1970 became my first published work.[13] Also exciting for me

---

13. Robert J. Barro, "Inflation, the Payments Periods, and the Demand for Money," *Journal of Political Economy*, 78, Nov./Dec. 1970, 1228–1263.

was that I learned later that Milton Friedman was the referee.

Bob Lucas and Rational Expectations

I was thrilled when Bob Lucas, my former colleague at the University of Chicago, was awarded the Nobel Prize in October 1995. Although it was 6:30 in the morning, Chicago time, I immediately called his home number. But, unfortunately, I reached his ex-wife, Rita (the number in my phone book dated back to my time together with Bob in Chicago in 1984). Apparently, I had woken Rita, but she recovered quickly to ask why I was calling Bob so early in the morning. I was worried that she would react negatively to the news of Bob's prize, but I told her anyway that I was calling to congratulate him on his award. Much to my surprise, Rita became very pleased and excited. Her first question was, however, even more surprising: "Did he get the prize by himself or with someone else?" When I said "by himself," Rita reacted with even more excitement.

I learned the next day that Rita's divorce agreement with Bob stipulated that she would receive half of any Nobel Prize that he won by 1995. Thus, I had unknowingly informed Rita the previous morning that she was richer by half a million dollars. Moreover, she had received this windfall at the last possible moment. No wonder she was so pleased, and no wonder she was so interested in whether the prize had been individual or joint. Fortunately, Bob was not annoyed with me about my inadvertent call to Rita, and his gracious comment to the press about his divorce agreement was, "A deal's a deal."

When I was on the economics faculty in Chicago, I had a sign in my office that said, "No smoking, except for Bob Lucas." It was worth enduring the smoke to talk to Bob but not to any other economist-smoker. This behavior accorded with my view that his selection for a Nobel Prize was a great idea, one that had been anticipated by most economists for several years.

Bob's contributions to macroeconomics in the 1970s permanently changed the very center of the discipline. Moreover, his influence has been as great on his critics, primarily Keynesians, as on his supporters, who tend to represent market-clearing or equilibrium-style approaches.

In some key articles published from 1972 to 1975, Bob applied John Muth's insights on rational expectations to monetary theories of the business cycle. Previous analyses had relied on simplistic Phillips curve models in which increased inflation led mechanically to lower unemployment and higher economic growth. But these theories assumed that workers and firms did not exploit readily available information and, hence, would commit the same mistakes time after time. For instance, higher inflation was assumed to raise workers' willingness to work because they were continually fooled into believing that their wages were worth more than they really were.

In Bob's theory, where expectations are formed rationally, people can be confused temporarily by monetary surprises. (Rational expectations are not the same as complete information or perfect foresight.) In particular, an unanticipated expansion of money and the general price level may temporarily fool workers into thinking that their wages had risen in real terms. Similarly, producers might believe that the prices of the goods they were selling had risen *relative* to the prices of other goods. Through these channels, a monetary stimulus might cause a temporary boom, but one that must end soon after the errors in expectations were recognized.

In the older-style theory, the permanent trade-off between inflation and unemployment meant that the monetary authority had a key role in fine-tuning the economy. The revised theory has dramatically different implications because monetary policy has its main influence when it is surprising. Thus, it is not enough to print more money when the economy is contracting and to print less when the economy is expanding. The expectations of this policy pretty much neutralize the real effects, a result that was demonstrated in 1975 in a major article by Tom Sargent and Neil Wallace.[14]

Unfortunately, the easiest way for a monetary authority to create surprises is to behave erratically, a policy that has effects that are real but harmful. Therefore, an important inference from Lucas's theory is that the central bank ought to relinquish the idea of fine-tuning and instead concentrate on the long-term objective of low and stable inflation. The Federal Reserve and other major

---

14. Thomas J. Sargent and Neil Wallace, "Rational Expectations, the Optimal Monetary Instrument, and the Optional Money Supply Rule," *Journal of Political Economy*, 83, April 1975, 241–254.

central banks had pretty much adopted this goal by the early 1990s, and this shift in policy has been highly successful.

As an aside, Bob's first theoretical paper on rational expectations, "Expectations and the Neutrality of Money," appeared in 1972 in a specialized publication, *The Journal of Economic Theory.* He had submitted this work to the American Economic Association's main journal, *The American Economic Review,* but it was rejected on the grounds of being too mathematical. In response, Bob expressed outrage and accused the editor of trying to run *Newsweek.* All of this was confirmed by the unfortunate editor, who asked me what I would have done in his position. My reply was that I would have accepted the paper at once.

The role of expectations is not limited to monetary policy but is crucial in many areas of economics, as Bob showed in his later research on investment, unemployment, taxation, public debt management, and asset pricing. In all of these situations, the appropriate evaluation of policy takes account of the way that expectations would be rationally formed. The older analyses, which failed to consider this adjustment of expectations, are now described as failing the "Lucas critique."

In the case of the Phillips curve, the critique means that the monetary authority cannot decide to expand money and prices during recessions and just assume that inflationary expectations will remain the same. Similarly, policies on taxation, transfers, and regulation will typically be anticipated and will therefore affect behavior. Such notions are commonplace in theories of corporate finance. No self-respecting finance economist would ever think that the government could change a policy that has an impact on financial markets, such as a tax on capital income or a charge on transactions, without affecting the way that assets are priced.

Aside from criticizing older methods of evaluating macroeconomic policy, Lucas showed how to develop models that encompassed the rational formation of expectations. These models are now used regularly by macroeconomists to assess alternative policies. Much of this research, now called real business cycle theory, has downplayed monetary factors and has focused instead on forces such as shifting technologies, changing patterns of international trade, and the government's fiscal and regulatory interventions. This emphasis on real forces also appears in recent research on the determinants of long-term economic growth, another area to which Lucas made major contributions.

Lucas likes to view his contributions not so much in terms of their implications for specific controversies in macroeconomics—the Phillips curve, the effectiveness of monetary policy, the validity of Keynesian models—but rather as part of an evolving methodology for the whole field of economics. He says in his *Models of Business Cycles:* "Dynamic economic theory . . . has simply been reinvented in the last 40 years. It is now entirely routine to analyze economic decision-makers as operating through time in a complex, probabilistic environment. . . . What people refer to as the 'rational expectations revolution' in macroeconomics is mainly the manifestation, in one field of application, of a development that is affecting all fields of application. To try to understand and explain these events as though they were primarily a reaction to Keynes and Keynesianism is futile."[15] Thus, for Lucas, a useful approach to macroeconomics involves the same economic modeling that would apply to corporate and public finance, industrial organization, and so on.

In the late 1970s, soon after I left Chicago (the first time in 1975), I invited Bob to present a paper to a seminar on macroeconomics that I was running at the University of Rochester. He was supposed to arrive the previous day, but I got a call from him that night. He had gone to O'Hare Airport in Chicago to catch his flight to Rochester, but he learned at the airport that the smoking section of the plane was already filled, so he went home. I tried to contain my anxiety while remembering all the people who were eagerly anticipating his seminar the next day, so I gently inquired whether he might be able to catch a plane in the morning. He said that he had already explored that possibility but that the only smoking seats available were in first class. I said that first class would be fine, and Bob came and gave a great seminar. Actually, I would have been happy to pay much more

---

15. Robert E. Lucas, *Models of Business Cycles* (Oxford: Blackwell, 1987).

than the extra airfare. (It is fortunate, with the abolition
of smoking on airplanes, that Bob is now a nonsmoker.)

Larry Summers, the Economist as Treasury Secretary and President of Harvard University

Until the early 1990s, Larry Summers was the consummate academic, always pursuing simultaneously more interesting projects than any reasonable person could keep track of. In 1991, Summers took leave from the economics department at Harvard to become director of research at the World Bank. Then, when Bill Clinton was elected president in 1992, Summers hoped to be named chairman of the Council of Economic Advisers. However, he did not receive this job offer, and the rumors at the time were that the appointment had been vetoed by the new vice president, Al Gore. Apparently, Gore was upset by Summers's unenlightened views on the environment, as evidenced by the famous memo that Summers had signed, but not written, while at the World Bank. This memo argued, with impeccable economic logic, that it would be mutually advantageous for rich countries to ship waste products to poor countries in exchange for substantial monetary compensation.

There was considerable irony in Gore's apparent blockage of Summers's appointment to the council. First, Summers was appointed instead in 1993 as undersecretary of the treasury for international affairs. Although the Treasury post may have seemed less attractive than the council chair at the time, Summers managed to build on the Treasury position to become secretary in 1999. Thus, Gore may have been unintentionally responsible for installing the best economist ever to be U.S. secretary of the treasury. (Alexander Hamilton had better intuition, but he lacked the formal training.)

A second irony involving Gore arose when Summers was chosen in 2001 to be president of Harvard University. Gore was apparently one of the alternative candidates but was dropped early on in the selection process. In fact, the head of the search committee, Robert Stone, was quoted in December 2000 in the *Boston Globe* as saying about Gore, "He'll go into our pool and be considered seriously. I rather doubt he'll get it. He doesn't have the academic and intellectual standing."

Summers's outlook on economic policy can be summarized by the remark that he gave me some years ago: "If I had your views on economics, I would find another profession." He meant that if free markets usually worked well and the government ought usually to stay out, then he would find economics to be an uninteresting occupation. Fortunately for Summers, he has always believed in the potential benefits from governmental activism, although the strength of this belief may have diminished over time.

He thinks that economic incentives and markets are powerful but that free markets often do not achieve socially desirable outcomes. Thus, the power of economic incentives becomes, for Summers, an efficient way for policymakers to influence choices, whether of saving rates or environmental pollution or jobs and wages. He believes that financial markets are especially subject to problems, including noise trading, irrational exuberance, and bubbles that sometimes burst. Summers is therefore supportive of strong governmental regulation of these markets, and he was once even sympathetic to an onerous tax on the turnover of securities.

Summers is fiscally conservative and supports budget policies that promote national saving and productive efficiency. Hence, he favors balanced budgets and funded plans for social security, including a role for private accounts. (However, this support for private accounts seemed to wane when he was secretary of the treasury.) Summers is—I would say unfortunately—a foe of the kinds of across-the-board tax cuts that Republicans are inclined to favor. For reasons discussed elsewhere in this book, I think that this opposition is a mistake.

Summers has a general tendency to favor capital levies, the term that economists give to taxes that fall on capital goods or other products of past decisions. The idea is that such taxes do not distort the economy, because earlier decisions cannot be undone. Hence, Summers tends to favor investment tax credits—subsidies to new capital—over reductions in corporate tax rates, which treat old and new capital alike. One problem with capital levies is that they cause serious distortions when businesses and households anticipate them. The inheritance tax is an example, because dead people find it hard to undo past decisions to avoid the tax. But high death taxes tend to be inefficient because live people know about them and alter their lifetime plans on saving and bequests accordingly. (I discuss tax issues more generally in section 4 of this book.)

As a policymaker, Summers was a positive force for free trade, the introduction of indexed bonds and the new dollar coin, and a hands-off policy toward the Federal Reserve's monetary policy. More problematic was his support of international bailouts, starting with the Mexican deal in 1995. These bailouts have involved an unfortunate alliance between the International Monetary Fund (IMF) and the U.S. Treasury. Subsequent problems in East Asia, Russia, Brazil, and Argentina have made the IMF and the Treasury eager to get out of the international bailout business. I think that these desires underlie the tentative and reasonable support that Summers offered for dollarization proposals in Latin America. The notion was that if Latin American countries fully used the U.S. dollar, then they would not be susceptible to the types of foreign exchange crises that they encountered previously.

Now Summers has become president of Harvard University. An interesting sidelight of this appointment was that it required a simultaneous academic appointment in a department. Therefore, without the extended debate that normally accompanies our deliberations, the economics department appointed him once again to be professor of economics. Perhaps we will be able to induce him someday to teach a course.

I am unsure what changes Summers will introduce at Harvard, but I am confident that he will go well beyond fundraising duties. It should be an exciting time, and I am glad that I will be around Harvard to see it. I just hope that he does not put me on too many university committees.

Bono, the Rock Star as Amateur Economist

My colleague Jeff Sachs does many interesting things, but I was surprised in the summer of 1999 when his secretary called to invite me to lunch with him and Bono, the lead singer of the rock group U2. Bono wanted to discuss the Jubilee 2000 campaign, a global movement aimed at canceling the international debts of the world's poorest countries. My first instinct was to decline, but I decided to check things out with my daughter, Lisa, who is an expert on rock stars. She said, "Dad, this is the coolest thing imaginable. I finally appreciate the fringe benefits from having a father who is a famous economist. Of course, you have to go." Since I never miss a chance to impress one of my kids, I went to lunch.

At the lunch, I said that I was an unlikely candidate to support Jubilee 2000 and that some left-wing economists would be much more promising. Bono said that was precisely why he wanted to talk with me. He wanted to see whether hard-thinking, conservative economists could be persuaded of the soundness of the campaign. In particular, he was not interested in another global welfare project, such as Live-Aid in the 1980s, but rather wanted to push debt relief as a way to promote sound economic policies. He even said that the relief would be conditioned on a country's commitment to use the freed-up money for productive investments in a transparent environment.

I was shocked to hear these kinds of arguments from a rock star. Nevertheless, I recovered sufficiently to say that this commitment would be unenforceable and that debt relief would not be on the top ten list of policies for growth promotion in poor countries. More important were well functioning legal institutions, promarket policies, sound investments in education and health, and macroeconomic stability. I mentioned the musical line "money for nothing" (from a song by Dire Straits) and said that it applied to a number of ways in which a country obtained unearned resources. These included debt relief, debt default, foreign aid, and even natural resources such as oil. Experience showed that all of these cases of free money tended to be harmful for economic growth. I also argued that growth would be encouraged if a country gained a reputation for honoring foreign debts and other agreements.

Bono agreed that it was important for a country to fulfill its debt obligations, especially those that originated from sensible commercial transactions. However, he and Sachs argued that most of the international debt of

African and other poor countries derived from poorly designed projects conceived by the World Bank, other international organizations, and donor countries such as the United States. Many of these loans had been made to corrupt dictators, who diverted the funds for personal gain. They noted that these debts could never realistically be repaid and that the overhang of interest payments prevented new international financing of sound investments. Bono said that the whole idea of the term *Jubilee 2000* was that it was a one-time happening and would therefore not encourage default on newly incurred debts. (I was a little worried here, because the Bible says that jubilees are supposed to occur every fifty years.)

Sachs was instinctively more sympathetic than I to the Jubilee 2000 campaign, because he has never thought that debt default did much damage to a country's reputation. Although not persuaded on this point, I was impressed when Sachs argued that we should assess the debt relief not so much from the standpoint of the borrowers, who would be getting money for nothing, but rather from the perspective of the lenders. These creditors, especially the World Bank and the International Monetary Fund, would be forced to write down their third world loans to realistic market values. This requirement might then encourage the international organizations to make future loans on a sounder economic basis.

By the end of the lunch, I was not convinced to put debt relief on the top ten list of growth-promoting policies for poor countries, but the arguments I heard were better than I had anticipated. Therefore, I was pleased at the time to offer two restrained cheers for Jubilee 2000.

In retrospect, this was two cheers too many. Bill Easterly has argued convincingly in his recent book that the problem of high foreign debt for poor countries is not new and that the remedy of debt relief is neither new nor effective. He says, "The problem of poor countries with high foreign debts is not a new one. Its history stretches from the two Greek city-states that defaulted on loans from the Delos Temple in the fourth century B.C., to Mexico's default on its first foreign loan after independence in 1827, to Haiti's 1997 ratio of foreign debt to exports of 484 percent."[16]

Despite this long history, the Jubilee 2000 campaigners regarded their quest as both new and promising. Yet Easterly says, "There is just one problem: the little recognition among the Jubilee 2000 campaigners, such as Bono, Sachs, the Dalai Lama, and the pope, that debt relief is not a new policy. . . . We have already been trying debt forgiveness for two decades, with little of the salutary results that are promised by Jubilee 2000."[17] He then demonstrates that the main response historically to debt relief has been for countries to run up new debts, most of which are used to finance nonproductive projects by corrupt governments. There is no evidence that past debt relief operations helped the poor, which were the

16. Bill Easterly, *The Elusive Quest for Growth* (Cambridge, Mass.: MIT Press, 2001), p. 123.
17. Ibid., p. 124.

intended target of Bono and his compatriots. So why
would one expect new debt relief to work any better?

Despite these doubts about Bono's policy proposals,
there is no question that the period since our lunch of
summer 1999 has been a remarkably successful time for
Bono in many respects. His campaign brought him into
contact with numerous world leaders, including President Bill Clinton and the pope (who is said to have tried
on Bono's famous sunglasses). Bono swayed numerous
politicians and economists to his cause, including the secretary of the treasury, Larry Summers, whom I have
already discussed. Even more amazing, Bono was as successful with conservatives, such as Senator Jesse Helms,
who hosted a Washington dinner for Bono in June 2001,
as with liberals. This great exercise in persuasion culmi-
nated in the $435 million debt relief legislation of Novem-
ber 2000. Moreover, despite all the time Bono spent
traveling and lobbying politicians, U2 produced in 2000
the brilliant album *All That You Can't Leave Behind*, after
an alleged dry spell in the 1990s.

In June 2001, Bono combined the Boston stop of his
Elevation Tour with the delivery of the Class Day speech
at Harvard's commencement (where he was made an
honorary member of the class of 2001). He, Sachs, and
Summers also spoke at a gala dinner that honored the
first graduating class of the Kennedy School's Center for
International Development, which gave Bono an honorary master's degree. He expressed appreciation to
Sachs, his frequent road companion on the debt relief

mission, and to Summers, who overcame his initial doubts to become a proponent of debt relief. Bono did, however, refer in his Class Day speech to Summers as culturally challenged, a remark that confirmed what Clinton had said in a speech that celebrated the passage of the debt relief law in November 2000: "I'll never forget one day Secretary Summers coming in to me saying, you know, some guy just came in to see me in jeans and a tee-shirt and he just had one name, but he sure was smart. Do you know anything about him? . . . So Bono has advanced the cultural awareness of the American political establishment, embracing everyone from Larry Summers to Jesse Helms. It's been a great gift to America's appreciation of modern music."[18]

I was surprised at the Kennedy School dinner when Bono asked to meet with me again, and I readily accepted his upcoming Boston event as the venue. After an amazing concert, which even I was sufficiently culturally adept to appreciate, we met at the hospitality suite of his hotel. Despite having just completed three hours of intense performing, Bono launched into a discussion of his new mission, which concerned the AIDS epidemic in Africa. U2's lead guitarist, The Edge, who was also soft-spoken and thoughtful, joined in parts of the discussion.

Bono said that he wanted to combine a push for medical assistance from rich countries with an expansion of

18. Reported on the Internet (www.j2000usa.org/updates/clinton6.html) by White House, Office of the Press Secretary, November 6, 2000.

international trade. Moreover, as with our earlier discussion about debt relief, he wanted to get an understanding of the conservative objections to his ideas.
(My accompanying daughter Lisa, who is still an avid
U2 fan at age twenty-six, said later that she could not
believe that the wondrous Bono sounded like her dad.
In terms of coolness, this is good for me but really bad
for Bono.)

In our discussion in Boston and in subsequent e-mail
exchanges, I agreed that the African AIDS epidemic is a
catastrophe, but I expressed concerns about the efficacy
of Bono's plan. It is true that the large pharmaceutical
companies have shown an inclination to yield to international pressures to provide AIDS drugs at low costs. Possibly this inclination stems from the willingness of
various governments, such as Brazil, effectively to steal
the property of pharmaceutical companies by abrogating
patents on drugs that treat diseases such as AIDS.
Regardless of one's view of the morality of this policy, it
is a bad idea to take the profitability out of the drug business, because any cure or vaccine for AIDS is likely to
emerge only from the efforts of profit-seeking corporations. The Brazilian government may be able to get away
with its theft of drug patents (because Brazil is a small
part of the world market for drugs), but the world as a
whole is better served by ensuring that successful drug
innovators receive high monetary rewards.

Another problem is that the rigorous routine
required for current AIDS treatments makes question-

able their effectiveness in low-income societies. Moreover, partial treatments can do more harm than good by increasing the prevalence of viral strains that are resistant to medication. If this is not enough, then one also has to realize that to the extent the treatments were effective, the resulting increase in life spans could— since the medicines were not cures—actually expand the epidemic.

I also mentioned that assistance might be more efficiently directed at measles and malaria—or, indeed, for providing safe drinking water—for which the dollar cost of saving a life was much lower. However, in order to say something positive, I noted that expanded international trade was a good idea and that it was politically astute to combine this economic orthodoxy with the proposed expansion of medical aid.

Because I hold Bono in high esteem, I wish I could believe that debt relief and assistance for AIDS would help to spur economic development and save lives in Africa. But my understanding of economics and my research on economic growth keep me from believing these things. I wonder what would happen if Bono instead directed his persuasive talents to further the classical liberal ideas that actually matter for economic performance. I have in mind property rights, the rule of law, free markets, and small government. And I would be happy to include investments in education and health. But, of course, this is just a dream. And the concert in Boston really was great.

Domingo Cavallo—The Second Coming of the Argentine Savior?

In the early years of the twentieth century, Argentina was one of the richest countries in the world. Then came many years of failed policies, and Argentina retreated to the status of a middle-income country. From 1913 to 1990, the average growth rate of per capita gross domestic product (GDP) was only 0.6 percent per year.

Things changed in 1991 when Domingo Cavallo (an economics Ph.D. from Harvard) took over as economy minister. Argentina implemented an array of promarket economic reforms, including a currency-board type of monetary system. This regime supported a fixed exchange rate—one Argentine peso was set at one U.S. dollar—and thereby promoted stability in inflation and interest rates.

However, on some occasions, such as the Mexican debt crisis and devaluation of 1994–1995, the financial markets speculated that Argentina would deviate from its one-peso-equals-one-dollar system. Anticipations of devaluation raised interest rates, because of increases in currency risk and in related default risk. Consequently, the Argentine economy tended to contract. Despite these difficulties, including the Mexican-induced recession of 1995, per capita GDP grew in Argentina at an average annual rate of 4.8 percent during the Cavallo years, which lasted until his ouster from the government of Carlos Menem in 1996.

The Brazilian fiscal crisis and devaluation of early 1999 caused more trouble because Brazil is Argentina's largest trading partner. The reduced cost of goods and services coming from Brazil created pressure for Argentina to respond with a devaluation of its own. This pressure was intensified by the worldwide strength of the U.S. dollar. Because of the one-to-one link of the peso to the dollar, the appreciation of the U.S. currency tended to raise Argentina's prices and wages relative to those in other countries. Hence, Argentina's tradable goods became less competitive, and Argentina also became less attractive as a place to invest. The market reaction is for Argentina's prices and wages to fall, but this deflation takes time, and economic contraction tends to occur in the meantime. This mechanism explains at least part of the drop in Argentina's per capita GDP by 3.2 percent per year from 1998 to 2000.

Early in 2001, President Fernando de la Rua's economy minister, Ricardo Lopez Murphy, failed when a reasonable program of curtailing public outlays hit a political roadblock. Out of desperation, the president turned to his political rival, Cavallo, to save the economy a second time. The initial reaction by many observers, including me, was positive. However, 2001 was not 1991, and Cavallo's proposals seemed to focus on confidence management with less of the brilliance and market orientation of ten years before.

The initial form of the program in spring 2001 can be understood as a reaction to two concerns: the size of the fiscal deficit and the overvaluation of the currency. Wary of the fate of Lopez Murphy, who was probably too outspoken in his proposals to cut spending for education, Cavallo seemed to emphasize higher taxes as the way to eliminate the deficit. The main new revenue device was a levy on financial transactions through the banking system. One problem with this approach is that the economy would benefit more from lower spending than from higher taxes. Cavallo did promise spending cuts eventually, but the forms of these cuts were unclear in the initial plan.

Another problem was that the new tax on financial transactions would soon be highly distorting. However, Cavallo hoped to generate a lot of revenue in the short run and then have the system evolve into a withholding tax scheme. An additional problem was that Argentina needed to boost its low level of investment by cutting the high tax rates on business income. Cavallo promised that these cuts would come, but the details were vague.

With respect to the currency board, Cavallo's proposals in spring 2001 tinkered with convertibility without abandoning it. He tried to devalue without devaluing by enacting a sharp rise in import duties on consumer goods. Then he proposed a complicated combination of duties on imports and subsidies on exports, all linked in a mysterious way to the exchange rate between the euro and the U.S. dollar. Basically, these policies amounted to clever forms of protectionism. The adverse consequences of protectionism are well known, and the announcement that the tariffs were temporary was not reassuring.

On the plus side, the elimination of most duties on capital goods was an important positive step. Another favorable element was that the new structure of import duties separated Argentina from its customs union (Mercosur) partner, Brazil. This change meant that Argentina, like Chile, would be able to negotiate on its own with the United States and other countries to form free-trade areas. Under the previous arrangements, where all Mercosur members had a common external tariff, Argentina would have had to depend on a deal that included Brazil. From a political standpoint, the chances of Argentina's successfully negotiating entrance into the North American Free Trade Agreement (NAFTA) or other free-trade arrangements are much higher if Brazil is not involved.

The fiscal outlook seemed to improve in August 2001 with the implementation of a zero-deficit law, which promised the quick elimination of fiscal deficits by means of drastic cuts in public expenditures. This law was a remarkable political achievement, and it seemed at the time to raise the chances for Argentina to weather its economic storm without any form of default or devaluation.

Since the economic reforms of 1991, Argentina had operated under two key principles for the public sector. The first was: *Do not devalue.* This principle was enshrined in the convertibility law, which created a type of currency board that fixed the value of the peso at one U.S. dollar.

Argentines knew that a failure of the currency board would imply the loss of external discipline for monetary policy. Without this discipline, the country would likely revert to the high and variable inflation that existed prior to 1991. The recognition of this inflationary prospect reinforced the credibility of the monetary regime, although it turned out not to be enough.

The second principle for the government was: *Do not default.* Obligations to bondholders were regarded as firm contracts that a serious country honored. Therefore, just as holders of Argentine money were led to believe that one peso was worth one dollar, so holders of Argentine bonds seemed to have reason for confidence that they would receive the contracted stream of payments from the government. For this reason, Argentina did not, until late 2001, regard reneging on its debt obligations as a satisfactory way out of its fiscal problems.

The fiscal deficit, although not exceptionally high as a ratio to GDP, fostered international speculation that one or both of Argentina's two core principles would be violated. In particular, the high interest rates faced by the government exacerbated the fiscal problems. This situation made public sector default more likely, even if the currency convertibility remained in place. To counter this speculation and ease the fiscal pressures, Cavallo used the zero-deficit law of August 2001 to introduce a third principle for the government: *Do not borrow.*

The new law limited public outlays over each quarter to the government's prospective receipts. Some of the adjustments in expenditures would even occur on a month-to-month basis. Thus, the government would not have to borrow on net from the financial markets and would "only" have to roll over outstanding bonds as they came due.

The planned size of the spending reductions was much greater than that proposed in March 2001 by the previous economy minister, Lopez Murphy. Although Lopez Murphy was ousted because of political opposition to his spending cuts, the various factions were persuaded by Cavallo in August to accept a more drastic plan. More remarkable still, the decreases in spending applied primarily to the most politically sensitive and difficult-to-control parts of the budget: wages and pensions. These outlays grew along with the unwise expansion of the government in recent years, and declines in private sector wages made public sector wages look especially high in a relative sense. Thus, both the form and size of the spending cuts made sense, but it is still surprising that the political consensus could be achieved.

Admittedly, there is a sense in which a continually balanced government budget is not ideal. Much better would be the option to borrow during bad economic times, such as recently in Argentina, and to run corresponding surpluses in good times. This "tax-smoothing" approach was, however, infeasible in the Argentina of 2001.

Things might have worked out better if Cavallo had implemented the new principle of budget balance when he replaced Lopez Murphy in March 2001. Sharp cutbacks in government spending may have been politically feasible at that time, but Cavallo seemed to underestimate the seriousness of the fiscal situation, especially as viewed by world financial markets.

The form of the convertibility law was another issue. In spring 2001, Cavallo moved to replace the U.S. dollar by a fifty-fifty dollar-euro basket as the anchor for the peso. However, this provision was to become effective only if the euro first appreciated to parity with the dollar. The last part confused me, because no one is able to forecast accurately future movements in the exchange rate between currencies, such as the euro and the dollar. Abstracting from this issue, I found understandable the inclusion of the euro in the basket, because Argentina's trade with the euro area is larger than that with the United States. Therefore, if one were starting from scratch to build a currency board for Argentina, then the fifty-fifty basket might be superior to the 100 percent dollar.

The problem, however, is that Argentina was not starting from scratch in 2001 and that the simple and clear convertibility law had been a key pillar of the country's enhanced credibility during the 1990s. Maintenance of this credibility was more important than the attainment of a somewhat better form of currency basket. In fact, the trade-off is exactly the one that Cavallo recognized in his adoption of the balanced-budget rule. Sometimes one has to give up features of a desirable policy (such as the ability to run budget deficits during recessions or include the euro in the currency basket) in order to maintain a higher degree of credibility.

Instead of changing the currency basket, my preference would have been to opt for a full dollarization, that is, for the full use of U.S. money in Argentina. Better still would be to negotiate with the United States to combine this dollarization with a free-trade agreement and with compensation for Argentina's conversion to the dollar (perhaps in the form of a supply of the needed dollar bills). Of course, these policies require support from the United States for freer trade and other sound economic reforms. The United States would benefit partly from expanded trade and partly from having to deal with fewer international financial crises. But whether this U.S. support would ever be forthcoming is uncertain.

After September 2001, the economic situation in Argentina deteriorated sharply. The recession worsened dramatically, driven partly by the downturn in the world economy after the September 11 terrorist attacks and partly by the budgetary stringency in Argentina. As a consequence, government revenues fell much faster than the cutbacks in expenditures, and the fiscal deficit widened. In his last official act, Cavallo froze the deposits in the banks, no doubt a symptom that the economic and legal systems were at the point of collapse. Shortly thereafter, Cavallo and the president, Fernando de la Rua, were out of office.

Through early 2002, Argentina had gone through a sequence of temporary presidents. The convertibility law was gone, the public debt was in default, and various gimmicks were being employed to redistribute the wealth of deposit holders, debtors, and bank owners. The government had returned to the printing press as a way to finance the budget, foreign investors were pulling out, and a principal focus was on persuading the International Monetary Fund (IMF) to send more money. It seemed that ten years of investment in establishing reasonable policies and government credibility were gone in a few months. Instead of guarantees about values of the currency, government bonds, and deposits, property rights had become dependent on the whims of incompetent public officials.

My best guess in early 2002 was that Argentina was headed back toward the hyperinflation and other failed policies that had plagued the country before 1991. Nevertheless, if a government were to appear that was able and willing to enact sensible reforms, there did still exist courses of action that might make things better.

My first suggestion would be a full dollarization of the economy, including the use of U.S. dollars as the currency. In 2002 in Argentina, a weaker arrangement, such as a currency board, could not possibly provide the credibility and discipline needed to reestablish a stable monetary policy. However, since a devaluation of the peso had already occurred, it seemed advisable to dollarize at the going market rate—roughly two pesos to the dollar—rather than attempting to return to the one-to-one parity. This devaluation would accomplish a reduction in Argentine prices and wages, relative to those in other countries. Then the full dollarization would prevent the return to hyperinflation.

The dollarization would require assistance from the United States or international institutions such as the IMF. The best form of this assistance would be a supply of the dollar bills needed to implement full use of the U.S. money in Argentina. An important complement for this assistance would be movement toward a free-trade agreement between the United States and Argentina. Other countries, such as Chile, could be included in what would amount to an expansion of the NAFTA arrangements.

Desirable domestic policies for Argentina include the freeing up of labor markets, with a related reduction in the power of labor unions. Also important is restraint on public expenditures, especially by the regional governments. Finally, the tax system should be changed to favor business investment. However, I am skeptical that much can be done to rekindle the confidence of foreign investors.

Al Gore in the Balance

Al Gore's humiliating loss of the 2000 presidential campaign, including the exquisitely excruciating verdict in

Florida, probably should have been enough to satisfy even his harshest critic. Nevertheless, in my earlier essay on Larry Summers, I already pointed out Gore's additional humiliation in the way he was rejected in 2001 by the selection committee for the Harvard presidency. So why am I about to criticize Gore yet again? I guess the reason is that I had to suffer through a reading of his outrageous book, *Earth in the Balance: Ecology and the Human Spirit* (Houghton Mifflin, 1992), and that memory compels me to show no mercy.[19]

The rise in oil prices during the 2000 presidential campaign served to highlight energy policy as an area of contrast between Gore and George W. Bush. Bush favored then—and still favors now—expansions of U.S. supply, including oil exploration in Alaska. The energy crisis in California and the terrorist attacks of September 11 have, I believe, increased support for this position. Gore emphasized reductions in energy demand, and he opposed Alaskan exploration on environmental grounds. He also argued that any expanded capacity would be delayed for five years and would therefore not help the current situation.

The last point is odd, because policymakers ought to value energy solutions even if they take five years to work. Moreover, investments that expand future oil supply would motivate producers, such as Saudi Arabia, to sell more oil earlier, while prices were still high. This

---

19. Al Gore, *Earth in the Balance: Ecology and the Human Spirit* (Boston: Houghton Mifflin, 1992).

reaction causes supply to rise and prices to fall before the new capacity arrives.

Gore's adamant opposition to oil exploration in Alaska, a position still embraced by most Democrats in the U.S. Congress, is important because it demonstrates an unwillingness to adopt a cost-benefit approach to the environment. Although such calculations can be difficult, we have to make these assessments explicitly or implicitly to make policy choices, and we will not make reasonable decisions if we always pretend that any environmental damage entails an infinite cost. The benefits of the exploration include a gross valuation of roughly $9 billion per year (assuming 1 million barrels per day at an average per barrel price of $25), starting perhaps in five years. Although much of the revenue would accrue initially to oil companies, the benefits extend ultimately to all users of energy. The cost involves hypothetical damage to a vast wilderness that is not especially attractive and that most of us will never see. I am waiting for the plausible calculation that makes this cost comparable to the billions on the revenue side.

Since Gore is reputed to be an environmental expert, it is curious that this area received little attention during the 2000 campaign. However, we can understand the policies that he represents by consulting *Earth in the Balance*. The book is striking for the extreme positions taken on all of the favorite environmental causes, including global warming, ozone-layer depletion, and preservation of endangered species and rain forests. The thesis is that we humans are unrestrained guzzlers of energy and dangerous enemies of the environment. Hence, enlightened policymakers ought to spare no effort (and expense!) in combating these tendencies.

This attitude led Gore to advocate abolition of the internal combustion engine within twenty-five years, by 2017. His view of automobile transportation was summarized as, "It makes little sense for each of us to burn up all the energy necessary to travel with several thousand pounds of metal wherever we go."[20] Thus, he believed that Americans' love affairs with their cars stem not from the efficiency and convenience of the mode of transport but rather from some sort of mass craziness.

Gore regarded the threat to the environment as so serious and imminent that he likened it to the Nazi Holocaust: "In the 1930s, when Kristallnacht revealed the nature of Hitler's intentions toward the Jews, . . . the United States and the rest of the world [were] slow to act. . . . Now, warnings of a different sort signal an environmental holocaust without precedent. . . . Once again, world leaders waffle. . . . Yet today the evidence of an ecological Kristallnacht is as clear as the sound of glass shattering in Berlin."[21]

Gore went on to compare the environmental danger to the injustice of American slavery: "Most . . . of the generation that wrote the Constitution were partially blind when it came to the inalienable rights of the African

20. Ibid., p. 326.
21. Ibid., p. 177.

Americans as slaves. . . . Today, most . . . are partially blind when it comes to our connection with the natural world."[22] Some people regard this sort of passion as admirable, but I regard it as reckless and offensive.

The hyperbole was hard to reconcile with Gore's support during the presidential campaign of the release of oil from the Strategic Petroleum Reserve. Apparently, during an election, moderating the rise in oil prices was more important than saving the world from holocaust and slavery.

From my perspective, the use of the reserve, although a political ploy that would have little impact on oil prices even in the short run, was a mixed bag. I always disliked the idea of the government's amassing the reserve—the main rationale was for use during wartime (when the government will likely keep prices from rising to market levels). The danger, as verified during the campaign, was that the reserve would be used for political purposes and to interfere with market forces. From this standpoint, the release of oil from the reserve was a good thing because it implied a smaller remaining stockpile and, hence, less potential for future manipulation.

It seems undeniable that Gore's views on energy and the environment were extreme relative to the opinions of average Americans. One therefore has to wonder why voters nearly elected him president in 2000. I think the reason is that most people who were familiar with Gore's views either doubted Gore's belief in his own extreme

---

22. Ibid., p. 276.

statements or expected the U.S. Congress to impose restraint. More realistically, however, the president has a lot of power to enact energy and environmental policies on his own. Therefore, it would have been prudent to take Gore at his word and regard him as a serious threat to carry out the mission described in *Earth in the Balance.* Fortunately, Gore became neither president of the United States in 2000 nor president of Harvard University in 2001.

George W. Bush and Compassionate Conservatism

Perhaps to demonstrate that my criticism of Al Gore does not reflect mere political prejudice, I have to include here some negative views on George W. Bush. I was particularly annoyed during the presidential campaign by Bush's self-description as a "compassionate conservative." More seriously, I am worried that his embrace of this term forecasts unwise expansions of government.

Milton Friedman began his classic book, *Capitalism and Freedom,* by citing the famous words from President John Kennedy's inaugural address: "Ask not what your country can do for you—ask what you can do for your country." Friedman complained that people spent too much time inquiring into the origin of the famous phrase and not enough on its substance. He then argued that neither half of the statement expressed a worthy relation between the state and its citizens. He said that the first part suggested that the government was the patron and the citizen the ward, whereas the second implied that the government was the master and the citizen the servant.

When I heard George W. Bush's less elegant expression, *compassionate conservatism*, I also focused initially on questions of origin. I noted first that many politicians in other countries had used similar terms, for example, "capitalism with a human face" in Chile, "social market economy" in Germany, "productive welfare" in South Korea, and "the third way" in the United Kingdom. All of these phrases represent an attempt to mix market-oriented ideas with political correctness. For some reason, politicians fear embracing, without apology, concepts such as capitalism, free enterprise, and conservatism.

Marvin Olasky's book, *Compassionate Conservatism* gives more information about the origins of Bush's phrase.[23] Apparently, the term began as a critical remark by Vernon Jordan in 1981 and was later used in a favorable light by a number of Republican politicians in the early 1990s. Olasky thinks that Bob Dole messed up the use of the phrase during his 1996 run for the presidency but that George W. Bush reinvigorated it as governor of Texas in 1997 and 1998.

I should have learned from Friedman's discussion of Kennedy that it would be more productive to concentrate on the substance of Bush's expression. Unfortunately, the substance is quite irritating, especially the word

---

23. Marvin Olasky, *Compassionate Conservatism* (New York: Free Press, 2000).

compassionate. The obvious implication is that ordinary conservatism is not compassionate and that modifications are therefore necessary. This is surely odd if one identifies conservatism with such basic principles as free markets, property rights, and limited government. As we have known since Adam Smith, the maintenance of these principles is the main reason that Western countries are successful. If one genuinely cares about the poor, then how can one not support the basic principles that create a nation's wealth? After all, the statistics across countries make clear that the most important determinant of poverty is a country's average income, not its degree of income inequality.

Although most of my unhappiness is with the word *compassionate,* I also do not care very much for the other word, *conservative.* This concept suggests maintenance of the status quo, even when that situation involves an array of unfortunate rules and overly activist government programs. It could also encompass forms of social conservatism that I find unattractive—for example, restrictions on abortion rights, enforcement of strict drug laws, curbs on immigration, and restraints on international trade. I much prefer the words *libertarian* and *classical liberal* (regrettably, the word *liberal* has been cleverly appropriated by the left in the United States).

Aside from the labels, one has to look at the specifics of policies. I am particularly worried that President Bush will support legislation that resembles the senior Bush's great intervention, the Americans with Disabilities Act

(ADA). This law epitomizes government policies that, although well meaning, tend to destroy incentives, harm businesses, and encourage wasteful litigation. This kind of intervention typifies the activist policies that were common in Western Europe in the 1960s and 1970s and that led to many years of economic stagnation. In the Netherlands, for example, overly generous disability policies led to almost 15 percent of the working-age population being classified by the end of the 1980s as state-supported disabled persons. Therefore, I would like to know whether a compassionate conservative would favor the ADA or favor its repeal.

To be fair, Bush has promoted a number of winning ideas that would appeal to classical liberals. One of these is personalized accounts for social security. The best line from Bush's acceptance speech for the presidential nomination was, "When this money is in your name, in your account, it's not just a program, it's your property." Also attractive is the president's zeal for cutting taxes.

I had once thought that Bush would strongly support school choice proposals. This idea uses solid classical liberal principles to design programs that would be of immense long-term benefit to the nation's poor. However, Bush has apparently caved in to the Democrats and abandoned school choice, at least for now. Is Bush being "compassionately conservative" in his education programs? I would say he is just committing familiar error in advancing big government, notably big government emanating from Washington, D.C.

Also troubling are Bush's ideas about health care. He talks about markets and incentives but seems mainly to embrace the Democrats' idea that government involvement should expand, for example, to add prescription drug benefits to the Medicare program. Is this compassionately conservative or just old-fashioned excessive government? I would say the latter.

All of this has to make classical liberals nostalgic about Ronald Reagan and Margaret Thatcher in the 1980s. On the one hand, one has to be concerned that these giants were followed by a succession of Bushes, Majors, Clintons, and Blairs. On the other hand, one has to be happy that the Reagan-Thatcher legacy was strong enough so that we can continue to prosper even under leadership that is merely compassionately conservative.

Joe DiMaggio

When Joe DiMaggio died in March 1999, I wrote this piece involving my childhood memories of the Yankee Clipper. Unfortunately, my editor at *Business Week* did not think it appropriate for a business magazine, and how can I disagree? I almost got it published in the sports section of a newspaper, but no luck. So, anyway, here it is.

Since Joe DiMaggio's death, even people who never saw him play baseball have reminisced about his life and the disappearance of heroes. My childhood memories of DiMaggio are, unfortunately, less positive. I was born in

the Bronx and therefore rooted for the New York Yankees since I first learned about baseball. My interest
began in 1951 at age six, when my family first acquired a
television set. This purchase enabled us to watch Yankee
games described by Mel Allen on WPIX, Channel 11. It
was DiMaggio's last season and also the rookie year of
Mickey Mantle.

What I remember of DiMaggio was an old guy who
could not move around very well and did not seem all
that great at baseball. In contrast, there was Mantle, a
godlike young athlete who seemed to have unlimited talent. I was annoyed that the old guy was getting in the
way of the young guy. Mantle seemed not to be getting
enough playing time, particularly in center field, which
he appeared to play much better than DiMaggio.

I remember watching one particular, fateful game,
where DiMaggio was in center field and Mantle was in
right. A soft fly ball was hit between them, and either
player could have handled the easy chance. But DiMaggio exercised his authority as the center fielder and called
for the ball. Mantle seemed to duck down to get out of
the way, so that DiMaggio could make the catch. But
after the catch, it became clear that Mantle had been hurt,
and I remember DiMaggio waving to the dugout for
help. The injury turned out to have been caused by an
exposed drainpipe, and it was the start of career-long leg
problems for Mantle.

Naturally, I blamed DiMaggio for the whole thing.
Why was he playing center field in the first place, when

he was obviously over the hill? Why was it not Mantle
who would call for the ball and avoid the injury that
would make him not so godlike?

I remember talking to my father at the time about my
feelings. I asked why the sluggish DiMaggio would not
step aside to let the amazing Mantle play. I remember my
father looking at me with an incredulous stare. No doubt
he had in his mind the past greatness and grace of
DiMaggio and could not comprehend how anyone, even
a six year old, would view DiMaggio as deficient. It must
be that he also knew that he could never convey this glo-
rious image of DiMaggio to his son. After all, I had not
seen anything before the 1951 season.

Looking at the statistics, I am unsure now why Mantle
seemed so good and DiMaggio so bad in 1951. It is true
that it was DiMaggio's worst season, where he batted
only .263 with a mere twelve home runs in 415 at bats.
But Mantle was not much better, with a .267 average and
thirteen home runs in 341 at bats. Maybe one player just
seemed to be on the way up and the other on the way
down.

I learned later that DiMaggio was one of baseball's
greatest players, with a lifetime batting average of .325
and the amazing batting streak of fifty-six games. But it
is one thing to read about this performance or see
replayed television clips and quite another to experience
the greatness while it is occurring. Thus, I can never quite
get out of my mind the image of the old guy who was
hanging on too long. Of course, even this is unfair,

because DiMaggio apparently realized full well that he had lost it in 1951, and he declined the Yankees' offer to return for the 1952 season.

Perhaps there is a contrast here with Michael Jordan's recent decision to attempt a second comeback in basketball. Maybe one reason most people remember DiMaggio fondly is that he stopped playing once he recognized that he could not perform at the high standards that he had achieved before. But, then again, I have never really understood the big attraction of going out while still on top. For most stellar performers, operating at substantially below their own historical best is still far superior to working in a different field or not at all. So why was it so great that Jim Brown retired from football while still on top, or that the Beatles and Simon and Garfunkel disbanded while at their best? The main consequence was that the public missed out on many years of fine, even if not the greatest, performance.

Things would have worked out a lot better if we had bought our first television set a year earlier, in 1950, so that I could have watched DiMaggio while he was still great. Then I could have shared with my father and other people the vision of the eternal baseball star. It might even have helped me to have more appreciation for some of my elders in the economics profession. But maybe I should be worrying instead about what the young hot shots in economics are thinking of me.

2   Economics of Social Issues

The Economics of Beauty

In times past, stewardesses were usually attractive women, and this arrangement added to the pleasure of many air travelers, usually men. By the 1990s, however, stewardesses had become flight attendants, who were much less likely to be attractive and were sometimes even male.

Many people view these changes as progress. Instead of pandering to the tastes of (straight) male customers, the airlines now largely ignore such worker traits as sex, age, marital status, and appearance and focus instead on serious qualifications (and seniority). Is it not a good thing if flight attendants are selected by job skills— meaning the ability to serve people well and to carry out safety procedures efficiently—and not at all on physical appearance?

I would say no. The only meaningful measure of productivity is the amount that a worker adds to customer satisfaction (and, hence, to willingness to pay) and to the happiness of coworkers. (A firm can pay lower wages to happier coworkers.) A worker's physical appearance—to the extent that this characteristic is valued by customers and coworkers—is as legitimate a job qualification as intelligence, dexterity, job experience, personality, and so on.

Almost everyone recognizes that severing the link between wages and intelligence would reduce efficiency or lower the national product. The reasons are that brain power would not be allocated to its most productive uses and investments in human capital would be discouraged. The outcomes are also unfair, in the sense that smarter people end up richer, and being smart is to a considerable extent a matter of luck. If one wants the government to redistribute resources from smart to stupid people, then one has to believe that the benefits from this redistribution exceed the resulting losses in national product.

The same reasoning applies to physical appearance. This trait is valued more in some fields than others, and restrictions on the dependence of employment and wages on physical appearance effectively throw away national product. The outcomes are also unfair, in the same sense as they are for intelligence. An interference with the market's valuation of physical appearance is justified only if the benefits from the redistribution of resources from beautiful to ugly people are greater than the losses in overall product.

Thus, it makes no sense to say that employment and wages based on physical appearance is a form of discrimination, whereas employment and wages based on intelligence is something else. The two cases are fundamentally the same.

Most people (and the law) accept this approach to beauty for some fields, for example, for movie and television personalities and modeling. Obviously, there would be a great loss of national product if the government were to dictate that Cindy Crawford had to be replaced by me in all of her commercials. But the difference between glamour fields and others in terms of the role of physical appearance is merely a matter of degree. If the government stays out, then the market will generate a premium for beauty, and this premium will depend on the values that customers and coworkers place on physical appearance in various fields. Probably the market will allocate more beauty to movies, television, and modeling than to assembly-line production and economic research. I have no idea how much beauty the unfettered market would allocate to flight attendant jobs, CEO positions, and so on. But—whatever the outcomes—why would one think that the judgments of government would be superior to the verdicts of the marketplace?

The legitimacy of beauty as a job qualification even for movies and television was challenged in the litigious 1990s. In a celebrated court case in 1998, a jury determined that Hunter Tylo was, despite being pregnant, sufficiently attractive to appear on the television program *Melrose Place*, although the producer thought differently. Personally, I have no opinion, but I would prefer to leave this judgment to voluntary exchanges between producers and actors rather than the court system.

Some solace can be taken from the 1997 settlement involving the restaurant chain Hooters. This agreement allowed the company to continue to limit its wait staff to attractive young women. Apparently, physical appearance remains legally as a "bona-fide occupational qualification" in this business. Of course, economic reasoning would imply that physical appearance is always a bona-fide worker characteristic as long as customers and coworkers think so.

A number of research studies have documented that beautiful people do better in life. Dan Hamermesh and his coworkers have used subjective information on appearance based on opinions of interviewers or of researchers looking at photographs.[1] A typical finding, based on a sample of over 3,600 persons (for the United States in 1971 and 1977 and for Canada in 1981), is that the wage differential between attractive and ugly people is around 9 percent for women and 14 percent for men. Some of these wage differentials may reflect characteristics that are correlated with physical appearance, such as health status and self-esteem, but the researchers found a similar beauty premium when proxies for these other traits were held constant.

---

1. See Daniel Hamermesh and Jeff Biddle, "Beauty and the Labor Market," *American Economic Review*, December 1994, and Daniel Hamermesh, et al., "Business Success and Businesses' Beauty Capital," National Bureau of Economic Research, working paper no. 6083, July 1997.

A study by Susan Averett and Sanders Korenman measures attractiveness by body weight and finds that obesity lowers wages by similar amounts for women (12 percent) and men (9 percent).[2] However, the adverse effects of obesity are substantially greater for women if one considers the probability of marriage (which obesity lowers by 25 percentage points for women and 14 percentage points for men) and the earnings of one's spouse (which obesity reduces by 25 percent for women and 10 percent for men). In these results, obesity may matter because of its correlation with other characteristics, such as health status and degree of self-control, rather than just for physical appearance.

All of these empirical studies seem to regard the relation between physical attractiveness and market outcomes as undesirable forms of discrimination, which would be nice for government policy to eliminate. For Averett and Korenman, the main regret is that public policies aimed at the elimination of labor market discrimination based on physical appearance—which might be attained with greater enforcement and broadening of the Americans with Disabilities Act (ADA)—would accomplish little. The problem is that discrimination in the marriage market has historically been much more important for women than discrimination in the job market. Perhaps these researchers should have recommended an extension of the ADA to the marriage market.

---

2. Susan Averett and Sonders Korenman, "The Economic Reality of the Beauty Myth," *Journal of Human Resources*, Spring 1996.

After all, what could be more unfair than the tendency of more attractive people to obtain better mates?

Standards of beauty vary across societies and over long periods of time. For instance, thin is beautiful in some settings, whereas pleasantly plump is more favored in others. Views on the attractiveness of age also vary. However, assessments of physical attractiveness seem to have a great deal of conformity for a given society at a given point in time, as documented by Elaine Hatfield and Susan Sprecher in their book.[3] The failure for standards of beauty to be universal across space and time does not, in any case, invalidate the argument that market valuations of beauty ought to be respected. The standards for physical attractiveness that apply in the United States in 2002 are the ones that matter today for people's self-assessed happiness. Unless we think that government officials know better than individuals about true happiness, the overall outcomes will be best if wages are allowed to reflect the current beauty standards.

A more difficult issue is whether beauty counts in a relative or absolute sense. For instance, if everyone were suddenly to become more attractive, as judged by current standards, would we all be happier? Or would we adjust the benchmark correspondingly upward and therefore be no happier? Height is an example of a trait

---

3. Elaine Hatfield and Susan Sprecher, *Mirror, Mirror . . . : The Importance of Looks in Everyday Life* (Albany: State University of New York Press, 1986).

that is mainly relative; little would be accomplished if everyone became one inch taller.

If people care about beauty in an absolute sense, then investments to enhance beauty serve a social purpose. However, if beauty is only relative, then these investments are socially wasteful, and the government could rationalize a policy to discourage such expenditures. This line of reasoning could support taxes on cosmetics, hair coloring, antibaldness treatments, breast implants, high-heeled shoes, and so on. But even in this case, it would be valuable to allocate beauty across sectors in an efficient manner, and, hence, it would still be reasonable for wages to reflect a beauty premium. Thus, more argument would be needed to expand the ADA to include ugliness as a socially protected disability. Perhaps the best idea is for the government to stay out of the beauty arena.

Abortion and Crime

Crime in the United States has fallen dramatically since 1991. By 2000, the homicide rate and the rate of total violent crime were each down by 44 percent. The rate for total property crime was down by about 50 percent.[4]

Many explanations have been offered for the increased safety, including higher expenditures on prisons and police, better policing strategies, the strong economy

---

4. See, for example, John Donohue and Steven Levitt, "The Impact of Legalized Abortion on Crime," *Quarterly Journal of Economics*, 116, May 2001, 379–420.

with its tight labor markets, and the diminished role of crack cocaine. However, each of these explanations turns out to be inadequate. For one thing, spending on prisons and police has been increasing since the 1970s, and this factor therefore cannot explain the timing whereby crime rose until 1991 and then fell sharply. Better policing methods, as touted by Mayor Guiliani in New York City, may matter. But crime rates also fell substantially in Los Angeles and the District of Columbia, which are not renowned for their policing skills. As to the strong economy, it is hard to show generally that growth in income and employment mean less crime. For example, the economy performed well from 1983 to 1989, while national crime rates rose. (Evidence across countries indicates that inequality of income, not the average level of income, is the main influence on crime rates.) Finally, the fall in crime rates after 1991 applies to places in which crack cocaine was never a significant factor.

A recent study by John Donohue of the Stanford Law School and Steven Levitt of the University of Chicago's economics department proposed a new causal factor for the drop in crime: the legalization of abortion in the early 1970s.[5] The idea is that the children who were not born would have been disproportionately more likely to grow up in poverty and on welfare with a young and poorly educated single parent. Because these factors are known to breed crime, the children not born would have been prime candidates to be criminals fifteen to twenty-five

---

5. Donohue and Levitt, op. cit.

years later. Hence, the absence of these children would contribute to the drop in crime rates since 1991. My reactions to this idea were: (1) This hypothesis is surprising. (2) This hypothesis may well be correct. (3) The implications are explosive politically and are likely to cause a major ruckus.

Donohue and Levitt presented three types of evidence to support their theory. First, the sharp expansion in legal abortions—from fewer than 750,000 in 1973 to a plateau of around 1.5 million since the early 1980s—fits with the timing of the drop in national crime rates since 1991. The cumulated effect from abortions fifteen to twenty-five years earlier can also explain why the national crime rate continued to fall through 2000 and is projected to keep falling for another ten to twenty years. In fact, the authors estimate that the number of abortions and the consequent reduction in crime would have been significantly greater had not the 1976 Hyde Amendment, which restricted federal funding of abortions through Medicaid, been in effect in various forms.

Second, a few states, including New York and California, legalized abortion by 1970, three years before the U.S. Supreme Court's *Roe* v. *Wade* decision in 1973. As the theory implies, the early legalizers experienced falling crime rates sooner than the rest of the nation. Finally, abortion rates responded to the legalization differently across states, and those with the highest rates of abortion in the 1970s experienced the sharpest drops in crime in the 1990s.

The researchers estimate that for every 1,000 extra abortions from 1973 to 1976, there were 380 fewer property crimes, 50 fewer violent crimes, and 0.6 fewer murders in 1997 (the last year that their studied considered). Overall, the abortion effect accounted for one-half of the drop in crime from 1991 to 1997. The rest is explained by increases in prisons and police and other factors or is unexplained.

About 20 percent of the abortion-related drop in crime arose because of the reduced population of fifteen to twenty-four year olds in the 1990s. However, the main effect is the reduced propensity to commit crime among the fifteen to twenty-four year olds in existence. Apparently, as hypothesized, abortion particularly weeded out the children who would have been likely to follow criminal careers.

Donohue and Levitt argue reasonably that they are carrying out objective scientific research about the determinants of crime and that the policy implications can be left to others. The effect on crime, even if confirmed by further study, would likely not moderate the views of pro-lifers, who view abortion as murder. (If abortion counts as murder, then the effect of abortion on total murder is strongly positive.) Similarly, the evidence would have little influence on pro-choice advocates, who already view a woman's right to an abortion as a fundamental liberty. However, for people with less extreme views, including myself, the policy implications could be important. If abortion rights turn out to be a strong crime fighter, then opinion is likely to shift in favor of these rights.

Colombia and U.S. Drug Policy

A few years ago, I went to Bogotá to speak on economic issues. I had nice discussions about the ongoing recession, fiscal imbalances, and the independent central bank's approach to reducing inflation and allowing the exchange rate to float. I also met the capable finance minister, Juan Carmilo Restrepo, whom some say may eventually become president.

Yet it was clear then and even clearer now that standard economic issues and the caliber of the country's economic advisers are sideshows in Colombia. The country's future is wrapped up in issues about guerrilla warfare, drug trafficking, political will to fight terrorism, and the efficiency of the military. It is a remarkable thing that the democratically elected president, Andrés Pastrana, effectively turned over the southern part of his country to a guerrilla group, the FARC (Fuerzas Armadas Revolucionarios de Colombia), to run as it pleases, mostly for the coca business. Pastrana would like to make peace, but the FARC have little reason to negotiate, because they have a good thing going with a compliant government.

In response to the disintegration of legal authority and the expansion of the drug trade in Colombia, the United States is supplying substantial funding for military and other purposes in support of Pastrana's "Plan Colombia." There are good arguments for the United States to counter an anarchic situation in an important country in Latin America. However, the commitment is dangerous and may eventually entail substantial U.S. military participation. Deputy Assistant Secretary of Defense Ana Salazar said early in 2000, "Each and every deployment order states . . . that DOD [Department of Defense] personnel are not to accompany host nation personnel on operational missions."[6] This promise sounds ominously like ones made early on in Vietnam.

One reason that the U.S. government is supporting Plan Colombia is that Pastrana is a friend of democracy and human rights. In fact, Colombia has long stood out in Latin America for its democratic traditions and limited political role for the military. Unfortunately, however, Colombia may now have too much democracy, with its constrained central authority and poorly functioning army, to combat the terrorist threat effectively. The country might be better off with a figure who resembles Peru's Alberto Fujimori of 1993—that is, someone who would be willing, temporarily, to suspend civil rights and democratic practices where necessary to defeat the guerrillas and reimpose law and order.

The U.S. aid to the Colombian government effectively puts the United States in the position of supporting both

---

6. Reported on the Internet at www.usia.gov/regional/ar/colombia/aid16.htm

sides in Colombia's civil war. The official aid goes to the government, and payments from American drug users go to the guerrillas. Perhaps instead of providing the official aid, we should work on curtailing the payments to the other side. This could be accomplished, virtually overnight, by legalizing drugs in the United States. People would still use drugs and pay for them (at lower prices), but the industry would no longer be connected to criminal activity at home and abroad.

The main U.S. drug policy has stressed curtailment of supply. Barry McCaffrey, who was head of the White House drug office in the Clinton administration, argued that Plan Colombia should be supported to achieve the antidrug successes of Peru and Bolivia. According to McCaffrey, "Without additional U.S. assistance, Colombia is unlikely to experience the dramatic progress in the drug fight experienced by its Andean neighbors."[7] Although Colombia has long been a major player in distribution, it became the world's largest grower of coca only recently, precisely because these activities became more difficult in the neighboring countries. There is no evidence that the antidrug successes in Peru and Bolivia curtailed the region's overall supply of drugs.

Colombia also experienced victories against the drug trade in the past by wiping out the distribution cartels in Medellín and Cali. But the response was a shift of the

7. Reported on the Internet at www.usia.gov/regional/ar/colombia/mccaf.htm

network to other groups and places. If Colombia experiences more such victories, then the drug business may return to its neighboring countries, including fresh possibilities in Ecuador, or to other parts of the world. The fundamental problem would remain the high willingness of drug users in the United States and other rich countries to pay. This demand would be serviced at some price, somewhere in the world.

One thing to notice is that we do not need Plans Colombia for countries that produce tobacco or alcohol. The important differences between tobacco/alcohol and cocaine/marijuana/heroin are not that one group of drugs is more dangerous than the other, but rather that the former is legal and the latter illegal.

We ought to be regulating and taxing the presently illicit drugs as we do tobacco and alcohol. We would not only raise tax revenues but would also save enormous resources now expended on police and prisons. The freed-up money could be used, in part, to fund health programs for drug users and educational programs designed to diminish the demand for drugs. Instead, we seem to be moving on an inexorable path on which tobacco will eventually be managed the way that we treat illegal drugs. Probably we would also be following this course for alcohol, except that we tried that before under prohibition, and it worked out badly. Overall, our drug policy is a mess, seriously in need of a basic reorientation.

SAT Scores and Meritocracy in Higher Education

President Richard Atkinson of the University of California caused a stir early in 2001 by proposing to eliminate the scholastic aptitude test (SAT I) as a required part of the college application. Opponents of the SAT have argued that the test is ineffective for evaluating applicants, but such claims have been largely anecdotal. For example, we now know that Senator Paul Wellstone of Minnesota had a stellar college career despite having an SAT score near the fiftieth percentile.

Given the wealth of available data, we do not have to rely on these stories. For example, every three years, the U.S. Education Department conducts the National Postsecondary Student Aid Study (NPSAS). This study provides information for a nationally representative sample of colleges on students' grade point averages (GPAs), admissions test scores (including the SATs and another examination, the ACT), and other family and school variables. Unfortunately, the study does not include high school grades. I have used the NPSAS studies for 1990, 1993, and 1996, which provide over 33,000 observations, to do my own analysis.

In this sample, admissions test scores have strong predictive power for college grades, although much of the individual variation in grades remains unexplained. If one takes account of many other factors (including college attended, race and gender variables, and parental income and education), then the t-statistic—a measure of how closely two variables move together—for the admissions test is 60. By way of comparison, researchers customarily regard a result as significant if this statistic exceeds 2. Therefore, admissions tests have strong predictive power for college grades. This predictive power is about as good in upper classes as for freshmen.

For given test scores and other variables, females have significantly higher GPAs than males of the same ethnic group (by 0.25). Blacks and Hispanics do significantly worse than whites of the same sex (by 0.24 and 0.08, respectively), whereas American Indians and Asians do not differ much from whites of the same sex. Another result is that the mathematics part of the admissions test is nearly twice as good as the verbal part as a predictor of college grades.

Results on the admissions tests were on average four percentiles lower for females than for males of the same ethnic group. Since women nevertheless had better college grades, they may have a legitimate complaint about admissions policies that rely on the SAT without allowance for gender. (However, it is possible that women have better grades because they tend to take easier classes.)

The same case cannot be made for the ethnic minority groups. After taking account of parents' income and education, admissions test scores for blacks were on average 17 percentiles lower than those for whites of the same sex. The comparable gap for Hispanics was four percentiles. However, as already noted, college grades for blacks and Hispanics were lower on average than those for whites, even if one compares students who had the same scores on the admissions tests.

The ethnic patterns in the admissions test results have sometimes been attributed to cultural bias. One problem with this argument is that test scores have similar predictive power for college grades within an ethnic group, such as blacks or Hispanics, as in the overall population. Moreover, other data indicate that test scores and college GPAs help to predict wages earned after college. Therefore, if the admissions tests reflect a cultural bias, then it must be the same bias that exists in other indicators of success that people care about.

Much of the opposition to the SAT seems to derive from the poor average performance of ethnic minorities, especially blacks. Clearly, a reliance on the tests conflicts with affirmative-action objectives, especially at the University of California, where explicit racial preferences have been ruled out. In fact, many people have expressed the suspicion that the dropping of SAT requirements is mainly intended as a way to get around the California law. In any event, the results from the NPSAS data do not support preferences for racial minorities as a way to maximize the academic performance of the student body.

A different argument that could be made is that the top schools should not be trying in any case to admit the applicants who will be the best scholars. An implicit assumption in academia is that the best faculty—indeed the best resources overall—should be matched with the most academically talented students. Some evidence suggests that the synergies from this matching are important, and, being a modest Harvard professor, I naturally find these arguments persuasive (though Harvard seems to be one of the worst culprits with respect to grade inflation). I am surprised, however, that the notion of partnering the best with the best has generated long-term support from voters and taxpayers in funding public institutions such as the University of California. After all, most voters and taxpayers (and their children) are not themselves the best, no matter how one chooses to measure that quality.

Perhaps the strong voter support for elite public universities is nearing its end, and the movement away from the SAT is a way of signaling the demise of the University of California's meritocratic status. But, somehow, I do not believe that President Atkinson had this idea in mind.

Napster, Prozac, and Intellectual Property Rights

What do Napster and proposals to limit prescription drug prices have in common? Both seek to reduce prices of goods that cost little to produce now but were expensive to create initially. Cutting prices today looks great for users and, arguably, for society as a whole. If it costs virtually nothing to copy a CD over the Internet, why should people not be able to copy and listen to the music rather than having to pay $15 at the local store? If it costs only a few dollars to produce and distribute a standard quantity of Prozac, why should people not be able to use the drug if they are willing to pay $10 rather than $100?

The problem is that the "high" prices are the rewards for the costly efforts that came long before. Music companies and artists expend time and money to create hits, and the bulk of the expenses are for failed projects. To compensate for these efforts and to provide incentives for future hits, the industry has to reap large profits on its few successes.

Piracy has always been a problem for producers of music and similar products, such as books, movies, and computer software. The incentive to abridge intellectual property rights reflects the big gap between the prices charged by the copyright owners and the actual costs of copying and distribution. Innovations in the Internet and computer technology have dramatically lowered these costs. On the one hand, these advances are desirable, because they allow products to reach a vastly expanded audience. However, the downside is the threat to intellectual property rights. These rights are partly a matter of fairness, in the philosophical sense that inventors ought to be able to control the use of their discoveries. But, more concretely, if intellectual property rights disappear and no other effective method of compensating creativity is adopted, we will see much less of future greatness in music, books, movies, and software.

It may be that the Internet makes impossible the effective enforcement of intellectual property rights in certain areas. If so, we are likely to be in trouble with respect to future creativity. However, the best policy for now would be to maintain the highest feasible degree of property rights, and the pursuit of the legal case against Napster was a helpful part of this policy.

Prescription drugs are similar in many respects, although the Internet has not yet figured out a way physically to copy drugs. However, the Internet may eventually lower significantly the costs of sale and distribution, once effective ways are developed to ensure the identity of the buyer.

One way to see that prices of patented drugs exceed current costs of production is to compare U.S. prices with the lower ones that prevail in some other countries. For example, Prozac sells in Canada for less than half its U.S. price. Some people infer that we ought to adopt Canada's single-payer policy for prescription drugs or, alternatively, allow reimportation of the cheaper goods back to the United States. A more reasonable view is that the incentives for drug research and innovation created by high U.S. prices give Canada, Mexico, and other small markets a free ride. That is, these small countries do not have to worry about the effects of their actions on the overall market and, hence, on the incentives for companies to develop new drugs. Unfortunately, the United States does not have this option. If the United States were to follow Canada's lead, then fewer new drugs would be available in the United States and the rest of the world.

Complaints about high drug prices are on the rise, and the irony is that pharmaceutical companies would be facing fewer attacks if they had been less successful at developing new drugs. The successful drugs of recent years include antidepressants, ulcer medications, agents to lower cholesterol levels, new types of antibiotics, and protease inhibitors to fight HIV. One would have thought that people would prefer the current environment with many effective new drugs at high prices to one with few or no new drugs at low prices. This choice is the relevant one for society, but many people fantasize that they can have low prices *and* many new drugs.

Particularly depressing (perhaps because I cannot afford Prozac) are current suggestions for "solving the problems" by subsidizing purchases of prescription drugs through Medicare. If we have decided (I would say wisely) not to reduce the rewards to pharmaceutical companies for effective drugs, then the question becomes, Who shall pay for them? Adding drug purchases to Medicare means that payment will come more from the general taxpayer and less from the typical elderly user. This shift might be defensible, despite the budgetary costs, if seniors were poorer than average. However, the opposite is now true, particularly because of the past expansions of social security and Medicare. This kind of proposal for additional public spending makes one yearn for the bad old days of budget deficits, when the attention was on effective ways to curb Medicare rather than on ways to expand it.

Microsoft and Antitrust Policy

In the capitalist system, which works better than any other known economic system, the reward for delivering good products at low cost is large profits. To secure these profits, businesses typically have to innovate in ways that lead temporarily to monopoly power over new products or methods of production. In a well-functioning free-enterprise system, businesses must be allowed to enjoy these profits. This incentive principle is well recognized in the patent system for inventions, as discussed for pharmaceuticals in the previous section. But the idea is much more general. Although it would be unwise to provide legal protection for most commercial discoveries, the government should not step in to limit profits at the first sign of monopoly power.

Yet sometimes, as with IBM in the past and Microsoft more recently, the government's response to too much business success is an antitrust action. The usual rationale is the benefits from competition in the form of lower prices and faster rates of product innovation. As a general principle, however, it is suspect to promote future innovation by limiting the reward for past successes. Moreover, the irony is that no sector has ever experienced as fast a rate of price decline and product improvement as the computer industry. Hence, the government's case against Microsoft was entirely hypothetical: if something was not done to limit monopoly power, then innovation would be constrained and future prices would be excessive.

The most compelling parts of the Microsoft case related to dominance of operating systems and the potential extension of this dominance to the Internet. These areas involved networks and industry standards, which feature important economies of scale. If the industry were static, these elements might form the basis for a single large company to capture long-term monopoly power and, hence, provide legitimate antitrust concerns.

However, the remarkable fluidity of the computer business has frequently been noted. No one has any idea about the form or role of operating systems five or ten years from now. Given this dynamism, any remedy that the government could propose for the current marketplace, such as insisting that Windows provide equal access for the no longer so popular Netscape Internet browser, would be unlikely to convey any net benefits to consumers. In fact, the government's intervention could be influential only if it locked in the industry's current structure, that is, only if it prevented the innovations that public policy was supposed to be promoting. Even more clearly, any breakup of Microsoft would cause far more harm than good.

The same kind of argument against antitrust intervention applied earlier to IBM and its supposed dominance of computers, even though the rate of innovation at that time was dramatically slower than it is now. The main beneficiaries from that eventually abandoned action were the many lawyers, economists, and other advisers who received handsome fees for their efforts.

A sad sidelight of the Microsoft case was the cooperation of competitor companies, such as Netscape (which was an independent company before its acquisition by AOL), Sun, and Oracle, with the government. One might have expected these robust innovators to rise above the category of whiner corporations, as represented in the past by Chrysler (in its pursuit of a public bailout in 1979) and Archer-Daniels-Midland (in its persistent lobbying for subsidies to ethanol). But a market-oriented economist such as me ought not to expect or even desire corporations to ignore private profit in order to further the public interest. The real problem is that whining can sometimes be profitable, because the political process makes it so. The remedy here requires a shift in public policies to provide less reward for whining, not changes in the basic attitudes of businesses.

One way to reduce these rewards is for the government not to pursue antitrust actions against the companies that win in the marketplace. Viewed in this way, Judge Thomas Jackson's findings in April 2000 against Microsoft and in favor of the company's breakup were disheartening. Much better was the District of Columbia Appeals Court decision in June 2001 that overturned the breakup remedy. Now it appears, despite the opposition of some state attorneys general, that the Microsoft case is headed toward a settlement with little teeth. And that is a good thing from the standpoint of the American consumer.

Personal Accounts for Social Security: Not a Free Lunch

During the 2000 presidential campaign, George W. Bush hit on a popular issue in his support for personalized accounts for social security. Given this popularity, it was surprising that Bush's opponent, Al Gore, initially opposed the whole idea. However, Gore recognized his mistake pretty quickly and then moved to propose a plan of his own. Because of this broad support, it is likely that some form of personal accounts will be approved during the current Bush administration. Therefore, it is worth examining some errors that usually accompany discussions of these systems.

One problem involves comparisons between the likely rates of return on personal accounts with those paid under the current setup. In general, any proposition that sounds like a free lunch opportunity to obtain higher rates of return involves some sort of fallacy.

Compare first the historical real rate of return delivered by the existing social security system—about 2 percent per year—with the risk-free yield of 3 to 4 percent that personal accounts could guarantee by holding inflation-indexed U.S. Treasury securities. The return in the existing program is only 2 percent because of the mechanics of a pay-as-you-go system.

Suppose that all workers contribute a fixed fraction of their incomes to social security. The key point is that today's contributions pay for the pension benefits of today's retirees, who were the previous generation of workers. The benefit that the typical retiree receives exceeds the amount contributed while working if the number of workers and the income of the average worker are rising over time. The total return corresponds to the growth of overall wage income. Thus, the real rate of return in an ongoing system is about 2 percent if the economy grows at that rate in the long run.

So why is it a fallacy to argue that the 3 to 4 percent yield on the personal accounts is better? The return is low in the existing system because workers start with a liability to provide for the retirees of the previous generation. The workers will get something back later from the next generation of workers, but the return is positive only to the extent of economic growth. If the workers could get out of their liability to the current elderly, they could earn a rate much higher than 2 percent, even if no personal accounts were introduced. But, of course, no one wants to reduce the benefits of the elderly. To put it another way, the personal accounts can pay 3 to 4 percent because they come, at the margin, with no obligation to raise pensions of the current elderly population. It is this feature—not the personal nature of the accounts and not any technical deficiency of the current system—that accounts for the differences in returns.

Another questionable argument is that the personal accounts can pay more than 3 to 4 percent, almost surely, by holding stocks. It is true that a diversified portfolio of U.S. stocks has yielded an average real rate of return of 7 percent, and this return has not been very risky over holding periods of ten years or more. It is therefore a puzzle why stockholders have demanded such a high-risk premium—historically around 5 percent—to hold stocks. Nevertheless, policymakers ought to accept the market risk premium as a guide. Otherwise, we might favor some truly strange policies, such as a requirement that households hold more stock than they currently choose for their personal portfolios. In a correct analysis, there is no free lunch gain from placing part of social security funds into stocks. The higher expected return is offset by at least the perception of greater risk.

The opponents of personal accounts have also committed logical errors. For example, it is erroneous to argue that the returns in the new system would be riskier than those available currently. In most plans, participants can choose to hold their funds in risk-free form, for example, to get an assured real return of 3 to 4 percent from inflation-indexed bonds. The risk on this holding is much smaller than anything confronting workers under the present retirement system, particularly when one factors in the political risk associated with the determination of future benefits.

One good reason to favor personal accounts involves property rights. Since the accounts would be owned by individuals, the pension benefits paid would be less subject to the political whims of future Congresses. However, this feature is threatened by proposals to reduce an individual's return from the current system in line with the amount received from the personal accounts. In this case, the property rights would be only partial.

Personal accounts also have an attractive element of choice. In most proposals, individuals can tailor their portfolios to their own preferences about risk versus return. These opportunities are unavailable under the existing one-size-fits-all arrangement.

Some advocates of personal accounts have gone further by arguing that the forced saving in these accounts would raise the national saving rate. The argument for an effect on overall saving is controversial theoretically and lacks clear empirical support. In addition, it may not be desirable to force people to save more than the amount they are currently choosing.

In the end, I favor personal accounts for social security not because of the possible saving boost or the claimed superiority of rates of return. For me, the crucial points in favor are those about property rights and choice.

3

Economic Growth, Democracy, and Things International

Eastern Germany—A Lesson in Welfare Dependency

With the unification of Germany in June 1990, people optimistically looked forward to rapid economic convergence of the backward eastern regions to the advanced western ones. This vision of quickly obtained equality was symbolized by the artificial one-to-one conversion rate that the German government established for part of the monetary assets held by former East Germans. This exchange (and the two-to-one rate that applied to holdings above a designated amount) represented a large gift to the eastern residents. According to the black market exchange rate, the economically appropriate conversion rate in 1990 would have been something like seven-to-one in favor of the western currency.

In some respects, the gift to the residents of the eastern regions was harmless and was just part of the price paid by western taxpayers for a successful takeover of the east. But more serious economically—and in the same mind-set politically—was the push for rapid wage parity in the two regions. This pressure stemmed partly from general notions of equality but mostly from the desire of West German labor unions to avoid competition from low-waged workers. Some West German companies may have colluded with the unions in order to avoid competition from the companies that would hire low-wage eastern workers.

The wage-equalization push has been largely successful. The first figure shows that wage and salary payments per worker in the eastern regions (excluding all of Berlin) were 49 percent of those in the west (including Berlin) by 1991 and then climbed to 75 percent by 1995. Since then the ratio has changed little, reaching 77 percent in 2000. In contrast, labor productivity (gross domestic product per worker) in the eastern regions (again excluding Berlin) was only 31 percent of the western level (including Berlin) in 1991, rose to 46 percent in 1995, and then changed little, reaching 48 percent in 1997–1998. Thus, convergence was less apparent for productivity than for wages.

These statistics on labor productivity derive from a concept of regional gross domestic product that is based on estimates of value added by region. These data are apparently available only through 1998. More recently, the German government has generated a new series, whereby gross domestic product (GDP) is estimated from payments made to factors of production, including labor. When labor productivity is computed in this new

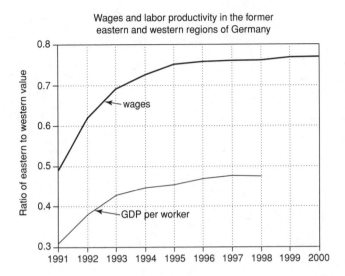

way, the resulting pattern for the ratio of eastern to western productivity looks much closer than the old one to the wage profile shown in the figure. In particular, the productivity ratio rises from 35 percent in 1991 to 65 percent in 1995 and 68 percent in 2000. Thus, it may be that the German government has solved part of the problem of lagging labor productivity in the eastern regions by measuring output in a different manner!

The second figure shows that the unemployment rate in the eastern regions of Germany (including the eastern part of Berlin but not the western part) has remained very high relative to that in the western regions (which include the western part of Berlin). The rate in the east reached 15 percent in 1992 and the still higher levels of 17 to 18 percent from 1998 to the start of 2001. In contrast,

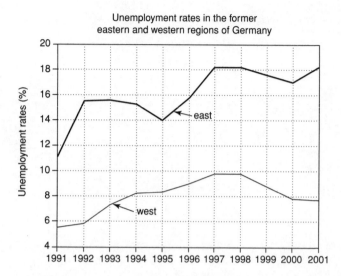

the unemployment rate in the west was a little over 5 percent in 1991, rose to around 10 percent in 1998, and was
between 7 and 8 percent for 2000 and the start of 2001.

It is unclear how much of the high unemployment in
the west—relative to that in the 1980s—derives from the
taxes and other burdens of the unification. Probably
much of the responsibility lies, as in France and much of
the rest of continental Europe, with ill-advised governmental regulations of labor markets. But more closely
related to the unification policies is the east-west gap in
the unemployment rates, which has remained throughout at around ten percentage points.

Incomes in the eastern regions have been sustained by
transfer payments, notably unemployment benefits. The
generosity of these benefits, combined with the union-

mandated excessive wage rates, likely explains the high unemployment rates in the east. One might argue that the main problem is the failure of the east's labor productivity to grow faster so that the gap between wages and productivity could be closed without reducing wages. The federal government has tried to help here by subsidizing businesses in the east, that is, by further intervention into the market process. This approach has not been very successful. The rise in GDP per worker in the east was rapid until 1993, but much of this can be explained as a recovery from the collapse of production that occurred with the unification in 1990. Since 1993, the growth in eastern productivity has been anemic, and the ratio of eastern to western productivity has been nearly constant.

The government's transfer and subsidy policies toward the east have slowed the migration of persons toward the west, partly by retarding eastern departures and partly by inducing westerners to move the other way. The total net migration from 1989 to 1999 was around 1.2 million or 7.3 percent of the 1989 population of East Germany. This number looks large but is only about half the total that I would have predicted based on economic fundamentals. Although this curtailment of net migration may be politically popular in the west, it retards the convergence process for labor productivity (which would have been helped by having more easterners working in the higher-productivity environment of the west).

Probably the catch-up of eastern to western productivity would have been more rapid with better—that is, less interventionist—public policies. But how rapid a rate of convergence could realistically be expected, even with more favorable policies? Some answers come from the histories of regions in European countries (including the former West Germany), the United States, Japan, and other places. The result derived from studies of these economies—sometimes described as the "iron law of convergence"[1]—is that poorer regions typically catch up to richer ones at a rate of 2 to 3 percent per year. According to this law, the level of eastern labor productivity should have reached 56 to 60 percent of the western level by 2010 and 68 to 76 percent of that level by 2030. Hence, the prediction is that it would take at least a generation for the productivity ratio to get close to the wage ratio—76 percent—that had already been attained in 1996.

The basic problem is that the German government ignored the iron law of convergence. It tried to engineer an almost overnight economic parity in the east partly by fiat and partly by massive transfer payments. Consequences of these policies for the east include the creation of massive unemployment and a likely permanent welfare clientele. Consequences for the west include large "solidarity" taxes

---

1. I originally heard this term, as applied to empirical findings from my cross-country empirical work on economic growth, from Rudi Dornbusch. But Larry Summers told me that Rudi got the expression from him.

and difficulties in dealing with political unrest in the east. Overall, it would have been better economically, and probably also politically, to rely more on market processes and less on government intervention.

Inequality and Economic Growth

Policies to promote economic development tend to fall into two categories: "hard" ones and "soft" ones. The hard group includes a disciplined monetary policy, which aims to maintain low inflation, and fiscal restraint, which entails low levels of public expenditure, efficient tax collections, low marginal tax rates, and effective public debt management. Also considered as growth promoting are openness to international trade, market-oriented regulatory policies at home, avoidance of military conflicts, and maintenance of a legal structure that promotes property rights and law and order.

Then there are the so-called soft issues. Included here are democracy (political rights and civil liberties), education aimed particularly at women, environmental protection, elimination of income inequality, and promotion of an array of civic organizations and "social capital." For most people, these soft issues represent goals that are intrinsically desirable. The contentious issue is whether these policies actually promote economic growth. The 1998 Nobel Prize in economics to my colleague Amartya Sen was viewed by some commentators as an endorsement of the softer road to economic development.

Recent research by myself and others has explored the consequences of one of the soft elements, income inequality, for economic growth. In the data, inequality tends to be highest in sub-Saharan Africa, notably South Africa, and in Latin America, including Brazil, Guatemala, Chile, Honduras, Peru, and Colombia. The lowest inequality is found in Europe, South Asia, and parts of East Asia, such as South Korea, China, and Japan. Some of the Anglo-origin countries—the United Kingdom, United States, Australia, and New Zealand— once had inequality close to that in continental Europe, but the degree of inequality has increased to some extent in these Anglo countries over the past ten to twenty years. The reason may be that these Anglo countries have been more willing than the western European countries to allow wages to reflect market forces, which have been driven in recent years especially by technological changes and globalization.

Economists have many theories about how inequality would affect economic growth, but the theories tend to have opposing predictions. For example, it is bad for growth if poor people lack the resources to invest in education. It is also adverse for growth if the disaffected poor tend to riot or steal. But inequality may enhance growth if concentrated resources are necessary for some investments and if the rich save a higher fraction of their incomes.

The empirical evidence since 1960 reveals little overall relation between the extent of income inequality and the rate of economic growth. Some countries with low inequality grew rapidly, such as Japan up to the early 1970s, South Korea, and Taiwan, and some grew slowly, such as most of South Asia and many of the member countries of the Organization for Economic Cooperation and Development in recent years. Some places with high inequality grew slowly, including much of sub-Saharan Africa and Latin America, and some grew quickly, such as Botswana (the star of economic growth in Africa), Brazil in the 1960s, and Chile since the mid-1980s.

There is a little evidence that inequality is harmful for growth in poor countries but conducive to growth in rich countries. Thus, there might be a growth-promotion basis for income redistribution in poor countries. However, the same reasoning suggests that policies to moderate inequality in the United States would diminish growth.

Some empirical patterns emerge concerning the evolution of inequality during the course of economic development. In the poorest countries, rising incomes tend initially to raise inequality, probably because a minority of the population benefits from entrance into modern sectors of production. However, once income exceeds roughly $2,000 per person, economic progress tends to reduce inequality. The implied inverted-U curve that relates inequality to average income is called the Kuznets curve, in honor of the Nobel Prize–winning economist Simon Kuznets, who was the founder of national income accounting.

Another finding is that primary education lowers inequality, whereas higher education raises it. Thus, a concern for inequality suggests a focus on widespread provision of elementary schooling in developing countries. However, this policy is unlikely to be growth promoting because the rate of economic growth turns out to respond more to education at the secondary and higher levels.

The bottom line is that growth promotion does not provide an argument for reducing inequality. The best thing that can be said is that the cross-country evidence does not reveal any conflict between higher growth and lower inequality, at least not until countries become rich.

Democracy in the New Congo?

The overthrow of Zaire's (now the Democratic Republic of Congo's) long-time dictator, Mobutu Sese Seko, had barely been accomplished in 1997 when the victor, Laurent Kabila, heard the standard Western clamor for democracy. The idea, apparently, was that the new leader should almost immediately hold multiparty elections and create a governing system that allowed for shared power. Interestingly, we are now hearing similar ideas expressed for the post-conflict Afghanistan.

The push for instant democracy in 1997 in the new Congo somehow seemed unfair. Was there to be no period of grace in which the person who deposed one of the world's worst dictators was to be rewarded with an interval of uncontested authority? What then was the reward for leading a risky revolution that eliminated the person who had led his country to more than thirty years of negative average economic growth? It is as though an entrepreneur had led a successful takeover of an inefficient company and was then told that he had to sell back his shares at the pre-takeover price and hold a vote to decide how the benefits of the takeover would be distributed.

In any event, "You have to be kidding" is the most appropriate response to the notion that Western-style democracy can be sustained in a country such as the Democratic Republic of Congo, where people have little education and in which per capita income is around $200. History makes clear that democratic institutions have little chance of survival when the standard of living is this low. For example, in all of sub-Saharan Africa, the poorest region on earth, the only place to have maintained a multiparty democracy for a long time is Botswana, which has been an exception to the usual pattern in many respects. (Unfortunately, instead of being an economic and political star, Botswana has more recently become exceptional in terms of the incidence of AIDS.) I expect that similar problems will emerge in terms of maintaining democracy or some kind of shared rule in Afghanistan.

The extent of African democracy has increased in recent years, partly because of Western pressure, and countries such as Nigeria and Mozambique have improved. But a realist has to look also at recent coups against elected regimes in other countries, including the Ivory Coast, Niger, Sierra Leone, and the People's Republic of the Congo. One also has to recall that the prospects for democracy in Africa looked better in the 1960s than they do now. However, the optimistic outlook in the 1960s was never realistic; it was mainly a romantic vision associated with the withdrawal of the European colonial powers.

Democracy, in the sense of political rights and civil liberties, is, in any case, not the characteristic of institutions that matters most for economic performance. There is some evidence that starting from the worst dictatorships, an increase in democracy is favorable, on average, for economic growth. To put this another way, although some dictators have delivered good economic results—Pinochet in Chile, Lee in Singapore, Fujimori for awhile in Peru, Park in South Korea, and the shah in Iran—the list of economic failures among dictators is larger: Marcos in the Philippines, Mao in China, Saddam Hussein in Iraq, Duvalier in Haiti, and a cast of despots in sub-Saharan Africa. The favorable economic effects from democracy seem, however, to disappear once a country attains a moderate degree of liberalization, such as that characteristic through the 1990s in places such as Malaysia, Mexico, and Turkey. Further expansions of democratic freedoms toward the Western ideal seem to come at the expense of economic growth.

This last finding is not surprising if one thinks of democracy as a setup in which decisions are literally made by majority vote. Such a system tends to favor redistributions from rich to poor and, more specifically, the expansions of social welfare programs that have typified and stifled Western Europe. These programs may have some desirable aspects, but they come at the cost of diluted incentives for investment, employment, and growth.

The government policies that are most favorable for growth include maintenance of secure property rights, promotion of the rule of law, fostering of free markets domestically and for international trade, macroeconomic stability, and investments in education, health, and some forms of infrastructure. Improvements in these areas are not necessarily accompanied by enhanced democracy, as is clear from experiences in Singapore, Chile, Peru, China, South Korea, Taiwan, and elsewhere. In contrast, there is a good deal of evidence that economic prosperity leads eventually to sustainable expansions of democracy. Even China, as it becomes wealthier, is likely to increase its electoral rights and civil liberties.

The best advice that outsiders could have offered Kabila, before he was assassinated in 2001 and then succeeded by his son, was not to focus on elections and power sharing but rather to emphasize the growth-promoting policies that could alleviate poverty. It might also have been a good idea for Kabila to commit more resources to personal security.

Chile's Presidential Election

Unlike many other presidential elections, the one in Chile in 2000 offered a serious choice of economic and social policies. Ricardo Lagos, the candidate of the ruling coalition, Concertación, promised a continuation of the mostly stand-pat center-left policies of the previous ten years. In contrast, the center-right candidate, Joaquin Lavin, would have extended the pro-market reforms of the 1970s and 1980s.

Since the mid-1980s, Chile has been one of the world's fastest-growing countries, despite the recession in 1999–2000. Its per capita gross domestic product (GDP) growth rate of 5 percent annually from 1985 to 2000 ranked among the top half-dozen countries in the world. Although income inequality is high in Chile, as in most of Latin America, the strong economic growth benefited the poor as well as the rich. This growth lowered substantially the fraction of the population living in poverty, even though indexes of the distribution of income did not change much. In addition, infant mortality fell from around 80 per thousand in the early 1970s to about 11 in 2000, and life expectancy climbed from sixty-four to seventy-five years.

Undoubtedly, Chile's outstanding economic performance derived from the free-market reforms instituted by the administration of General Augusto Pinochet from 1973 to 1989. Despite his contributions to economic and social conditions, Pinochet remains one of the most hated targets of the world's leftists. Some of this antipathy derives from the general's poor human rights record, especially in the 1974–1976 period after the coup against President Salvador Allende. The crimes of these years did not seem necessary for preventing revolution and therefore cannot be justified as part of a war effort. However, the abuses also do not stand out among dictators, and Pinochet ought to receive credit for peacefully relinquishing most of his authority in 1989. I think that the extent and durability of the leftist animosity toward him reflects the very real economic success; no one has done more than Pinochet and his economic teams to demonstrate the superiority of free-market capitalism over socialism.

Until 1998, Chile had dealt reasonably well with the conflict between Pinochet's human rights failures and his economic successes. An amnesty law allowed the country to achieve sufficient consensus to consolidate democracy without destroying the pro-market economic system. This consensus was disturbed by the propensity of the administration of President Eduardo Frei to prosecute retired generals for crimes of the 1970s. Further trouble came in London in October 1998 when Pinochet was arrested on the request of an out-of-control Spanish judge, who was tacitly supported by Prime Minister Blair of England. The Frei government should have regarded this detention as a warlike act that threatened the sovereignty of Chile. Instead, the Chilean government responded with only mild objections. Fortunately, a Chilean panel of judges decided in 2001, after Pinochet had been returned to Chile, that the former general could not be tried for his alleged crimes because of his poor health.

Lagos's economic program was summarized by his motto "growth with equality" (a phrase that unfortunately reminds me of George W. Bush's "compassionate conservatism," as discussed in the first section of this book). The main idea was to maintain the core of the economic reforms that were accomplished under Pinochet, while chipping away at the edges by adding new labor market regulations and mild social welfare programs. Thus, the policies would not cause great economic harm but would also not lead to further economic improvements.

Lavin's idea was to strengthen the economy by finishing the job of reform. One possibility, which Lavin promised not to pursue without labor's support, was to begin the last major remaining privatization project, the massive state-owned copper company, Codelco. But the most exciting possibilities involved dramatic expansions of the use of the market in the health and educational sectors. Somehow it seemed appropriate that Chile, the country that led the way in privatization of social security, would also show the world how to use markets to improve the quality of health care and of primary and secondary schooling.

Maybe Chileans should have made their choice in the presidential contest solely on the basis of the candidates' educational backgrounds. In Lagos, they got a Ph.D. in economics from Duke University, whereas in Lavin, they would have gotten a master's degree in economics from the University of Chicago. So the question was, What is better: a Ph.D. from Duke or a master's from Chicago? Personally, I thought the choice of Lavin was pretty obvious. However, the electorate thought differently and chose Lagos in a close vote. Who am I to question the wisdom of the people?

Mexico's New Democracy

Probably no one in Mexico had more at stake in Vicente Fox's 2000 election as president than the outgoing leader, Ernesto Zedillo. The clean and peaceful transfer of power from the incumbent party, the PRI (Partido Revolucionario Institucional), to the PAN (Partido Acción Nacional) allowed Zedillo to claim a competitive democracy as his main legacy to Mexico. Although the autonomous electoral authority had been created by Zedillo's predecessor, Carlos Salinas, Zedillo deserves credit for allowing the electoral authority to function. He also enacted campaign finance reform (at vast taxpayer expense), introduced an open presidential primary within his own party, and permitted an actual change of power through the voting process. The world would never have regarded Mexico as truly democratic until the PRI lost the presidency at least once since its founding in 1929. (In any event, I have always been puzzled as to how the Partido Revolucionario

Institucional could be revolutionary and institutional at the same time.)

The expansion of democratic rights, while attractive in its own right, provides no reason to raise one's assessment of Mexico's long-term economic prospects. These prospects depend on economic and legal reforms, which are areas in which Zedillo made little progress. Admittedly, Mexico has been growing fast since 1996; gross domestic product growth averaged 5.5 percent through 2000. However, the rapid pace of economic activity has been driven mainly by export growth, which reflected the movement toward free trade under the North American Free Trade Agreement (NAFTA) and the strong U.S. economy. Indeed, the Mexican economy slowed at the beginning of 2001, along with the U.S. economy.

As with most of the other important economic reforms in Mexico, the opening to international trade occurred in the early 1990s under the administration of Salinas and his finance minister, Pedro Aspe. In addition to NAFTA, there was a series of privatizations and deregulations, progress in macroeconomic stabilization, improvements in fiscal management and discipline, and the introduction of personal accounts for social insurance.

Zedillo's record of economic reform was comparatively weak. The main success was the continuation of the push for free trade, including agreements with the European Union and several countries in Latin America. Otherwise, the principal initiative was the introduction of private financial management for the existing personal social insurance accounts.

In terms of omissions, Zedillo can be criticized for doing little on privatization, especially in the energy sector; for making no progress outside of electoral reform in reducing corruption in government; for permitting the crime problem to worsen, notably in Mexico City; and for allowing the banking system to become a burden on taxpayers and a nonparticipant in investment financing. Many of the problems in the banking sector derive from the massive devaluation at the start of Zedillo's administration and from the bailouts that followed that crisis.

One area that Fox ought to pursue is privatization in the electricity business. Even more significant would be privatization of the petroleum sector, but progress here may be politically impossible, and Fox has already indicated his intention to maintain government control. Mexico, like Venezuela, seems to regard public ownership of oil as critical for national pride.

Also important would be enhanced competition in telecommunications, another area in which Zedillo failed to make progress. In the banking sector, the main promise seems to lie in further infusions of foreign investment in an environment where the government refrains from future bailouts. The 2001 buyout of Banamex by Citibank is a very promising development.

Fox plans large public expenditure programs on elementary education and rural infrastructure. These programs could be productive but are likely to create serious fiscal pressures. These ambitious spending plans therefore increase the importance of improving revenue collections by reducing tax evasion. Fox also has to deal with Zedillo's unfinished business with regard to corruption and crime.

On the macroeconomic side, it is important to create a stable long-term approach to monetary policy. Mexico has a sort of independent central bank that appears to want to promote low inflation while allowing the exchange rate more or less to float. However, monetary policy seems, in practice, to be driven by short-run considerations involving financial sector liquidity rather than rules related to inflation, exchange rate maintenance, or targets for interest rates or monetary aggregates.

Mexico might benefit from a full-scale dollarization in which Mexico fully adopted the U.S. dollar as its currency (and likely received U.S. financial compensation for making the switch). The large and growing integration of the Mexican and U.S. economies makes Mexico an excellent candidate for dollarization, which is an issue that I discuss more fully below.

Dollarization in Russia?

In the summer of 1998, I was vacationing comfortably on Cape Cod. In August, just after the Russian government defaulted on some of its bonds, I received a call from a Russian businessman. He asked me to come to Moscow to consult with some government officials on their economic problems. The situation was dire, he said, and they desperately needed economic insights from experts who had previously not been a part of Russia and its problems.

About a week later, I stepped into the twilight zone of a meeting at a Russian ministry. The discussion began when a government adviser stated that President Yeltsin's attempt to reappoint Viktor Chernomyrdin as prime minister was about to be turned down by the Russian parliament, the Duma. He said that the usual procedure was to resubmit the nomination a couple more times but that they were considering, instead, suspending the Duma and installing the new prime minister by fiat. Then he asked what I thought of this idea. Hence, a few days after lying on the beach on Cape Cod, I had plunged into a potential Russian coup.

I said that the proposal was interesting but that my expertise was more on economic issues. Looking somewhat disappointed, the Russian adviser agreed to shift the meeting to economic topics. Henceforth, we dealt with issues that were more boring but also safer than those raised at the outset.

The economic and political risks in the Russia of August 1998 were evident, but it also seemed that the turmoil might create opportunities for basic institutional changes. At times of crisis, drastic changes in policies sometimes become politically feasible, and it was therefore worth considering reforms that might otherwise be unthinkable. That was why we discussed a currency board as a basic change in Russia's monetary institutions. The discussion included Domingo Cavallo, who was also at the Moscow meeting. (Cavallo, whom I discussed in the first section of this book, was, in 1998, Argentina's former minister of the economy.) Cavallo was terrific in his advocacy of a currency board, because he was able to give a vivid description of how such a regime had been implemented in 1991 in Argentina amid an atmosphere of economic crisis.

Under a currency board, the Russian central bank would limit itself to exchanging the ruble for foreign currency at a fixed rate. Since large quantities of U.S. one-hundred-dollar bills were already circulating in Russia and since many domestic transactions were viewed in dollar terms, the natural unit would be a new ruble that equaled one U.S. dollar. In 1998, the euro was not functioning, so the alternative of linking the ruble to the euro was unavailable. (In 2002, it might be that the euro would be the preferred anchor currency for Russia.)

The central idea of a currency board is to eliminate exchange rate volatility and hyperinflation as threats to the economy. The experiences in Argentina in the 1990s and other countries (such as Hong Kong, Bulgaria, Estonia, and Lithuania) have shown that this system can work. A currency board is guaranteed to fix the exchange rate if the central bank begins with international reserves at least equal to its liabilities—mainly currency and bank deposits—and if these reserves are dedicated to conversions between the domestic and foreign currency at a specified rate. The setup does rule out an independent monetary policy. Some economists view this as a short-coming, although an independent monetary policy is, at best, a mixed blessing. In fact, a strong point of a currency board is that it prevents the central bank from financing the government, bailing out banks, providing credit to favored economic sectors, propping up the domestic stock market, and so on.

In a working system, the Russian government would foster the idea that the ruble was as good as the dollar by not restricting the uses of foreign currency as media of exchange or stores of value. Since tax collections and other items would remain ruble denominated, the domestic currency could eventually emerge as the preferred means of payment for most transactions inside the country. In this happy state, people would choose to exchange their hoards of U.S. currency for ruble-denominated assets, and the central bank would receive income (called seignorage) from the issuance of ruble currency.

The currency board period should be preceded by an interval of floating exchange rates during which the value of the ruble would be determined by the market without public intervention. This market value would depend on expectations about future policies, including whether Russia was thought to be moving toward the currency board system. The confidence in this regime switch would be raised by the presentation of a coherent economic plan, which included the implementation of a currency board.

It is crucial to recognize that a currency board is not a cure-all. It must be combined with an effective economic team and a broader program that includes fiscal discipline, legal reforms, and improvements in the banking system. Unfortunately, the Russia of August 1998 lacked both the economic team and the coherent economic program. Perhaps as a consequence, the plan for Russia that Cavallo and I had advocated was not carried out. In fact, all of the public officials whom I met in August 1998 were no longer in power a short time afterward (although one of the economists now seems to be the chief economic adviser for President Vladimir Putin). This shift in power may also explain why my one-time assignment as a major economic policy adviser to Russia proved to be short-lived. But maybe in the future I will get another urgent call to action while lying on a beach somewhere in the world.

Yankee Imperialism in Asia

Before the 1997 financial crisis, the fast-growing economies of East Asia were favorites of economists and international investors. Especially hard hit with currency devaluations and high interest rates were South Korea, Malaysia, Thailand, and Indonesia. Forty-year periods of sustained high growth were replaced in 1998 by sharp economic contractions, ranging from 7 percent in South Korea to 15 percent in Indonesia. What has happened since? Are the reforms and economic recoveries strong enough so that investors should rush back into these four crisis countries?

The recovery has been impressive in South Korea, with growth averaging 9 percent per year for 1999–2000 but receding during 2001. Reasonable, though less brisk, recoveries also occurred in the three other countries.

Other signs are less favorable. The four crisis countries had been known for high rates of saving and investment, with ratios of investment to gross domestic product in 1997 ranging from 30 to over 40 percent. These values collapsed by 10 to 15 percentage points during the financial crisis and have not rebounded significantly through 2001. Although the earlier levels of investment were probably excessive, the failure of investment to recover suggests that businesses do not anticipate returns to the sustained high growth rates of the past.

This impression is reinforced by stock market prices, which had not reattained the U.S. dollar values of 1996 by late 2001. Thus, the stock markets also point toward lower growth. The obvious comparison is with Japan at the end of the 1980s, where the collapse in stock market prices accurately signaled more than a decade of subsequent growth at anemic rates.

In a conference that I attended in 2001 in South Korea, economists from the International Monetary Fund and elsewhere discussed possible policy changes that might improve the economic outlook. My suggestions led some participants to label me as a "Yankee imperialist," though I naturally regarded these charges as unfair.

My first ideas were about the banking sector. Although economically important, this sector has been a recurring source of problems for many middle-income countries. In South Korea, the banks are now predominantly government owned and run, an environment that is not promising for growth promotion and efficient allocation of credit. Nevertheless, the government has been dragging its heels on privatizing the banks, especially with regard to sales to foreigners. Up to 2001, only one sale of a bank to a foreign company had been completed. This resistance to foreign ownership is a mistake, because foreign-owned banks offer a number of advantages to a middle-income country.

First, a foreign company with substantial assets would withstand the kinds of disturbances that have led in the past to bank failures. Second, the government would have limited ability to pressure a foreign-owned bank to lend money to favored sectors, such as the large business groups (*chaebol*) in South Korea. This immunity to pressure is favorable for the economy but may explain the reluctance of many governments to encourage foreign ownership. Finally, the government would not be inclined to bail out a foreign-owned institution. Knowing this, the institution would have to be prudent in its lending practices.

Asian countries could learn in this context from Mexico. With Citibank's purchase of Banamex in 2001 and the earlier buyout of two other institutions by Spanish companies, the three largest Mexican banks will now be run by strong foreign institutions. Because of these changes, Mexico's banking sector finally looks promising.

Another issue in South Korea is the too-big-to-fail doctrine, which had been applied in the past to the chaebol. More recently, the government has been willing to allow the market to decide which businesses will survive, as was clear with the failure of the Daewoo Corporation. However, this policy seemed likely to be tested again, as the government in 2001 was providing assistance to some of the troubled parts of the Hyundai Corporation.

Finally, I suggested that South Korea consider relinquishing its own currency by adopting the U.S. dollar, that is, by dollarizing. (I discussed possible dollarization for Argentina before in my essay on Domingo Cavallo, and I will discuss more general issues about dollarization later.) One advantage of dollarizing for South Korea is that it would avoid the kind of currency crisis that occurred in 1997–1998. Although South Korea would have to abandon an independent monetary policy, such independence has always come at a cost. Moreover, unlike Argentina, which experienced problems with its currency board from 1998 to 2001 because of the strong U.S. dollar, South Korea is linked fairly closely to the United States in terms of trade and other dimensions. Another favorable element is that dollarization could be combined with negotiations on freer trade with the United States and on U.S. compensation for South Korea's costs of supplying U.S. dollar bills.

My proposal for dollarization in South Korea, combined with my endorsement of foreign buyouts of banks, led to the Yankee imperialism charge. As to dollarization, my main defense is that the U.S. dollar is an attractive money, although for some other countries, such as those in Eastern Europe, the euro would be a more natural currency to adopt. As to foreign ownership of banks, it is fine if companies from rich countries other than the United States end up providing the assets and experience to run part of the Korean banking system. In any event, the more serious issue is whether I am correct that these policy changes would improve the economic outlook and thereby justify the return of investor enthusiasm for South Korea.

Dollarization and the Grand Ecuadorean Experiment

In 1947, there were 76 independent countries in the world; today there are 193. Until recently, most countries had their own currencies. Hence, the expansion of the number of countries led to a proliferation of the number of currencies.

Individual currencies are valued partly for national pride and partly because they allow each country to pursue its own monetary policy. However, the benefit attributed to independent monetary policy has diminished as central banks have learned to value low and stable inflation over active macroeconomic stabilization. Moreover, the expansion of world trade has made it increasingly inconvenient for each country to have its own money.

Therefore, the identification of currencies with countries has weakened, and the discussion has shifted toward one of desirable currency unions.

Roughly sixty small economies have been members of currency unions for some time. Examples are the fifteen-member CFA Franc zone in Africa; the seven-member Eastern Caribbean Currency Area; the use of the U.S. dollar by Panama, Bermuda, and the Bahamas; the use of the Belgian franc by Luxembourg and the Swiss franc by Liechtenstein; and the use of the Israeli shekel in the West Bank and Gaza.

The most important example of a recently formed currency union is the twelve European countries that use the euro. Other countries will likely sign on later, though Denmark said no and the United Kingdom is still deliberating. Dollarization has been contemplated by several countries in Latin America, including Argentina, Peru, and much of Central America. In particular, El Salvador has moved toward full use of the U.S. dollar. Argentina and some other countries have gone part of the way toward dollarization through their adoption of currency boards. However, as I have already discussed, Argentina abandoned this system in 2001.

From a scientific standpoint, the most exciting recent development is the dollarization in 2000 by Ecuador, a country that has been an economic and political disaster for some time. The situation appeared to brighten in 1998 with the election as president of Jamil Mahuad, who had been a successful reformer as mayor of Quito. However, he was unable to assemble the political support needed to deal with problems of the public finances, subsidies on consumer goods, foreign debt, and the banking sector. When bank runs occurred in March 1999, he responded by freezing deposits. This action, apparently as dubious legally as it was economically, eventually earned him an arrest warrant after he moved to the United States.

Mahuad proposed dollarization in Ecuador in January 2000 not as part of a coherent economic package, but because he became desperate to do something dramatic when his approval rating fell below 10 percent. Although the proposal was well received, it was not enough to save Mahuad's presidency, and he was soon ousted in a bloodless coup. However, his vice president and successor, Gustavo Noboa, recognized the potential popularity and efficacy of dollarization and therefore moved aggressively to make the U.S. dollar the currency of Ecuador. The transition was nearly complete by September 2000. No doubt, the process of obtaining the U.S. dollars needed to replace the Ecuadorean sucres was aided by the high price of oil, Ecuador's main export.

There is an ongoing debate on whether major monetary reforms, such as dollarization, can be successful without preconditions, especially sound fiscal and banking practices. Ecuador is therefore interesting because none of these preconditions existed. In fact, these deficiencies were part of the crisis atmosphere, and the crisis generated the political consensus to do something drastic: dollarization. In other words, the lack of supposed preconditions explains why dollarization occurred in Ecuador. (In contrast, El Salvador is in much better shape in overall economic policy, and the dollarization announced in 2000 had been contemplated for many years.) The crucial question for Ecuador is whether, once in place, dollarization helps to cure other problems, such as fiscal imbalances and banking inadequacies, so that the missing preconditions become fulfilled postconditions.

One attraction of dollarization is that sound monetary and exchange rate policies no longer depend on the intelligence and discipline of domestic policymakers. The monetary policy is essentially the one followed by the United States, and the exchange rate is fixed forever. (One temporary problem, caused by the sharpness of the devaluation in Ecuador prior to the dollarization, is that inflation for 2000 was very high. However, the inflation receded in 2001.)

As of 2001, dollarization seemed to be serving in Ecuador as a foundation for the resolution of other economic problems. Progress had been made with international debtors, and some domestic reforms had been accomplished. My prediction is that dollarization will continue to help with these problems, although political impasses will sometimes occur. In any event, many economists, including myself, will be looking closely to observe the outcomes of this grand experiment.

My Brief Tenure at the World Economic Forum

After false starts in some previous years, I finally made
it in 2000 to the World Economic Forum (WEF) in the
picturesque ski town of Davos, Switzerland. One of the
program's major themes was globalization, particularly
the role of international flows of goods, credit, and technology. President Bill Clinton and Prime Minister Tony
Blair expounded on this topic and attracted huge
crowds, but the prize for insightful reasoning on free
trade clearly went to President Ernesto Zedillo of
Mexico. In fact, his talk was so good that I have been
forced to upgrade my assessed value of a Ph.D. in economics at Yale.

Zedillo referred correctly to the beneficial effect of
trade openness on economic growth, but observed, also
correctly, that other policies were crucial. These include
domestic free markets and privatization, macroeconomic
stability, investments in education and health, and institutions that sustain the rule of law.

Zedillo described as "globaphobes" the unholy coalition of interest groups that now campaigns actively
against free trade and globalization. These groups, which
had disrupted an earlier meeting of the World Trade
Organization in Seattle and tried unsuccessfully in 2000
to do the same in Davos, include labor unions in rich
countries, environmental crazies, and extremists of the
left and right. He particularly criticized the growing ten-

dency to attack free trade under the banners of labor standards and environmental protection.

Poor, low-wage countries can compete particularly well internationally in the export of goods that require a lot of unskilled labor. If rich countries force poor countries to provide U.S.-style wages and working conditions, then the poor countries will be much less able to compete and will therefore be denied a means to grow and eventually attain U.S.-style wages.

International cooperation on environmental regulation is sometimes reasonable, but this argument provides no reason to restrict international trade. If anything, the growth induced by expanded trade tends to generate structural and policy changes that increase the protection of the environment.

In contrast to Zedillo's tough talk about globaphobes, Clinton's speech in 2000 to the WEF pandered to these groups: "We don't have very well-developed institutions for dealing with the social issues, the environmental issues, the labor issues . . . that's why people are in the streets; they don't have any place to come in and say, okay, here's what I think." Since U.S. labor unions and environmental activists are not lacking in voice, Clinton must have been referring to a lack of representation for the left- and right-wing extremists.

I did see a lot of celebrities in Davos. The meeting had more than forty presidents or prime ministers, not to mention some really important people, such as Bill Gates,

Michael Dell, and the 1999 Nobel Laureate in economics, Robert Mundell, whom I discussed in the first section of this book. I had to conclude, however, that I lacked the Davos spirit, because I rapidly lost interest in country leaders, not to mention lowly U.S. senators or governors or mere finance ministers or central bank heads. Truth is, my biggest thrill was passing through the security lines manned by the machine-gun-toting Swiss security forces (who were highly successful in ensuring that the Davos gathering did not repeat the anarchy of Seattle).

One thing that remained unclear was the purpose of the World Economic Forum. Businesses, which pay the freight, send representatives to see and perhaps influence the many politicians who attend. The politicians come mostly because they want to talk to other politicians. (The organizers have ingeniously created a self-fulfilling equilibrium in which the rational expectation is that the other politicians will come.) Of course, the politicians also appreciate the presence of the many journalists, who participate because of the politicians.

Academics come as well, partly because they like to rub elbows with celebrities and partly because they enjoy expense-paid vacations in pleasant places. (The Saturday night soiree was especially memorable.) The presence of the academics seems intended to allow the politicians and journalists to pretend that they are participating in scholarly interaction. However, very little of the World Economic Forum involves serious scholarship.

For me, the celebrity thing and the pleasantness of Davos were not enough to compensate for the long journey. Anyway, I fortunately did not have to decide whether to attend the meeting in 2001. After I published a critical commentary in *Business Week*, the organizers of the WEF must have forgotten to invite me. A similar slight applied to the 2002 meeting in New York. Now that was an extravaganza that I could not have resisted. Maybe I should be more careful about publishing critical remarks.

What to Do with the International Monetary Fund?

Personnel changes at the IMF (International Monetary Fund) and proposals for changing the IMF received a lot of attention in 2000. After a lengthy public debate, the leading countries settled on the second proposed German, Horst Köhler, to replace Michel Camdessus as the fund's managing director. Unfortunately, the circus-like process began to resemble an affirmative action procedure when it became clear that a particular nationality, German, was a prerequisite for the job.

Calls for changes at the IMF came in the report from Congress's International Financial Institution Advisory Commission, led by the economist Allan Meltzer. (I was a witness before the commission on issues related to inequality.) The Meltzer Commission's report surprised me by not calling for the abolition of the IMF: "The Commission did not join the council of despair calling for the elimination of one or more of these institutions." However, it came close to recommending abolition by proposing a new IMF that would be limited to short-term liquidity assistance to solvent economies, collection and publication of data, and provision of economic advice.

The short-term loan facility could be useful, but the worry is its resemblance to the IMF's role under the Bretton Woods regime that prevailed until the early 1970s. That role expanded greatly in the 1990s, and it is unclear how this mission creep would be avoided under the new regime. If the fund retains access to lots of money, then it is politically difficult to say no to large, insolvent countries, such as Mexico in 1995 and Russia in 1998. Hence, past mistakes in the form of too much lending would likely be repeated, and the elimination of the IMF might have been a better choice. The recent large loans allotted to Argentina and Brazil seem to confirm this pessimistic view.

I agree that the IMF's collection and distribution of data have been useful. An advisory role might also be satisfactory (and some of my friends and former students perform these tasks admirably). However, this function could be served as well by nongovernmental institutions. In any event, the demand for the IMF's economic advice is likely to be low if this advice were no longer tied to qualifications for loans.

Also surprising was the commission's call for the IMF to join the Jubilee 2000 campaign for writing off the debts of heavily indebted, poor countries. (This campaign was championed by the rock star Bono, whom I portrayed in the first section of this book.) Probably this provision was part of the compromise needed to secure the eight-to-three vote in favor of the commission's overall report. This type of debt forgiveness amounts to a form of foreign aid in which the recipient gets the money only by following bad policies that fail to achieve sustained economic growth. Foreign aid has, in general, a poor record of promoting prosperity, and this type of aid is sure to have worse effects.

Admittedly, debt forgiveness has the virtue of forcing the IMF to own up to the low market value of much of its loan portfolio. Hence, the Jubilee concept might not be bad if some mechanism prevented a repeat of the process through new loans that would eventually again be forgiven. The commission proposes that the IMF no longer make such loans, but I would not bet on the implementation of this idea.

Since the commission's proposals to shrink the IMF are unlikely to be adopted, the managing director will likely continue to be one of the world's most important financial officials. Köhler's principal credentials, aside from being German, include his role in the economic unification of the two Germanys. Given the terrible miscalculations here, as I discussed earlier, it is hard to regard this experience as a plus. However, given my own supposedly difficult personality, I found irresistible the adjectives that people have applied to Köhler:

irascible, autocratic, too demanding, does not suffer fools gladly, bad tempered, difficult management style, and others. At least these words were accompanied by more positive ones, such as *smart, forceful, strong willed, and hardworking.*

The irony is that the IMF had available the ideal candidate in its deputy managing director, Stan Fischer. Fischer, formerly an economics professor at MIT, is not only an outstanding economist but has a pleasant and effective management style, combined with experience at the fund. He also seemed ideal on political grounds, because he was born in Africa, previously held a British passport (related to his residencies in the former British colonies of Northern and Southern Rhodesia), and now holds a U.S. passport. Apparently, Fischer's shortcoming was that the British passport was not enough to make him European and was surely not enough to make him German.

In any event, by summer of 2001, Fischer had tendered his resignation, and his replacement by Anne Krueger of Stanford University had been announced. One thing I know is that Krueger will be strong enough to deal with Köhler. Whether this all signals better policies ahead for the IMF is yet to be seen.

4

Fiscal Policy,
Monetary Policy, and
the Macroeconomy

Budgets and Tax Cuts

In November 1980, the Reagan Revolution began with his election. It was the one time that I was really excited with presidential politics and the one time that I was eager to serve in Washington as an economic adviser. Naturally, I was disappointed when no one asked me, but I am still pleased by most of the policies and results.

The two keys to the Reagan fiscal policy were lower tax rates and reduced public expenditures. Since Reagan did better on the first part than the second, this policy resulted in budget deficits. But the deficits turned out not to be harmful to the economy, despite popular opinion to the contrary, and they helped politically for holding down the growth of government. Since the cuts in tax rates stimulated private spending for investment and consumption, the cuts contributed to the sustained economic growth from 1982 to the end of the decade. The combination of this growth record with the sharp lowering of inflation and interest rates was a great economic success story. Yet Republicans became shy about taking credit for this success, and they even supported the ill-advised tax increase engineered by the first President George Bush in 1990. The further increase in tax rates in 1993 under the Clinton administration came despite Republican opposition.

After George W. Bush's election as president in 2000, the political winds shifted again in favor of tax cuts. Much of the changed sentiment stemmed from the projected federal surpluses, which—until the recession and war of 2001—seemed to be large enough to make retirement of the publicly held federal debt a realistic possibility. The situation reminded me of a long-ago fiscal episode.

"In January 1835, the national debt was paid off; the existence of a surplus was an assured fact . . . What was to be done with it?"[1] At that time, when Andrew Jackson and then Martin Van Buren were the presidents, the problem of ongoing surpluses was "solved" mostly by increasing federal spending. Part of the added expenditure went through the states, as directed by the Distribution Act of 1836. Other parts were spent on public works and fighting Indians in Florida. There was no tax cut, despite some suggestions to reduce tariffs. However, the recession of 1837 helped to reduce government revenues (which came at that time mostly from tariffs and public land sales).

---

1. Davis Dewey, *Financial History of the United States,* 11th ed. (New York, Lougmans, Green, 1931), p. 219.

The worry about running out of public debt had not been an issue for 165 years. However, Federal Reserve chairman Alan Greenspan revived the matter in 2001 in testimony before Congress, when he pleased Republicans and shocked Democrats by declaring himself a tax cut advocate. According to Greenspan, "The emerging key policy need is to address the implications of maintaining surpluses beyond the point at which publicly held debt is effectively eliminated."[2] He then argued that reduced taxes were better than added expenditure as a way to resolve the quandary of insufficient public debt. Of course, the depletion of the stock of publicly held government bonds could be avoided by allowing the social security trust fund to invest in a broad class of securities, including corporate stocks. However, this option would be politically less worrisome if the funds were held in personal accounts rather than in a government-managed portfolio. Political pressures relating to the composition of the government's portfolio could become a problem.

A number of other arguments, more compelling than public debt depletion, supported the case for tax cuts in 2001. One is to lessen tax distortions and thereby stimulate investment and long-term economic growth. Decreases in marginal tax rates are especially attractive, because they increase incentives to work, save, and invest. From this perspective, the exactly wrong kind of tax cut is the 2001 rebate, which gave people money

---

2. Testimony before the Senate Budget Committee, reported in *The New York Times*, Jan. 26, 2001.

independently of the taxes they had paid (as long as they paid some taxes). This change gives out money without reducing anyone's marginal tax rate.

Another good argument is that tax reductions remove revenues from Washington, D.C., and thereby keep the Congress from spending them. Reagan well understood this point when he pushed for income tax cuts in the early 1980s. The resulting budget deficits of the 1980s and early 1990s pressured the U.S. Congress to hold down federal spending. For example, during the mid-1990s, the government was seriously considering substantial cuts in Medicare, including raising the age of eligibility to sixty-seven. However, when the surging U.S. economy replaced budget deficits by surpluses, the Congress shifted its interest to expansions of Medicare, including new benefits for prescription drugs. From the perspective of encouraging fiscal discipline by removing money from Washington, the tax rebate of 2001 may not be so bad.

Although the long-term perspective should be paramount, it may sometimes be desirable to have a tax cut to offset a recession, such as in mid-2001. Certainly the recession-fighting promise of the tax changes seemed to help politically in getting the cuts through Congress. To fight a recession, however, the Bush plan should have been changed to eliminate the gradual phase-in of tax rate cuts. Otherwise, the expectation that future tax rates will be lower than current ones contributes to the economic downturn by motivating the postponement of production and work. This feature of the 1981 tax reform may have contributed to the 1982–1983 recession. Therefore, it was a little surprising to see this mistake repeated during the recession of 2001. But no doubt it is too much to expect that the U.S. government will learn from past economic experience.

September 11 and the War on Terror—What Does it Mean for the Economy?

In late 2001, there was still a lot of uncertainty about how the terror of September 11 and the resulting war in Afghanistan would affect the U.S. economy. The early reactions from commentators and financial markets were sharply negative and suggested that the United States, and perhaps the entire world, would plunge into a deep recession. However, I thought that these views were wrong. In fact, I thought that the oft-mentioned parallel between the terrorists' attacks on the World Trade Center and the Pentagon and the Japanese attack on Pearl Harbor also applied in the economic realm. Thus, a key economic point is that the U.S. entrance into World War II at the end of 1941 was followed by a boom that shook off the remaining economic problems from the Great Depression. Of course, this economic perspective does not mean that World War II was a net benefit to the United States, and the same goes for the terror of September 11.

My strategy for analyzing the economic effects of the war on terror is to think of this action as analogous to

U.S. wars of the past. The main conclusion from this analysis is that the overall impact will be expansionary by 2002 and will therefore help the economy recover from the slowdown that began toward the end of 2000.

If we consider World War II, Korea, and Vietnam, then we have examples of large, medium, and small wars. In World War II, peak military spending in 1944 was 60 to 70 percent of the prewar gross domestic product (GDP).[3] During the Korean War, spending peaked at around 11 percent of GDP in 1952, and during the Vietnam War, it peaked at about 2 percent of GDP in 1968. The evidence is that economic activity expanded during each war but by less than the amount of wartime spending: my estimate is that each $1 of military outlays led to an increase in GDP by 60 to 70 cents. To put it another way, while military spending raised output, there was no free lunch. The spending had to be paid for by decreases in other forms of spending or by more work effort. It turned out empirically that the decline in other spending showed up especially in private investment.

The effect of the Gulf War is harder to isolate, because military spending rose by only about 0.3 percent of GDP. The economy was in a recession in 1990 before the war started in January 1991. Economic growth resumed by the second quarter of 1991 but remained low until 1992.

---

3. I really mean that it was 60 to 70 percent of an estimate of what prewar GDP would have been if the economy had been operating at normal capacity. The actual GDP in the late 1930s was less than this amount because the economy had not yet recovered fully from the Great Depression.

The estimate from the other three wars suggests that little of the recovery stemmed from the war itself.

For the current war on terror, if we sum up the likely near-term added expenditures for the military, domestic security, and reconstruction of New York City, we get at least 1 percent of GDP. This calculation is likely to underestimate the added wartime spending because we will probably also see a long-term reversal of the "peace dividend" that derived from the end of the cold war. During the Clinton administration, from the end of 1991 to the end of 2000, defense outlays fell from 6.2 percent of GDP to 3.8 percent (and the number of military personnel declined by around 1 million to reach a total of less than $1\frac{1}{2}$ million).

Given the insecurity of the post–September 11 world, I would expect a permanent increase in defense spending. If the United States responds as it did during the Reagan defense buildup of the early 1980s, defense spending would rise by 1 to $1\frac{1}{2}$ percent of GDP over a one to two-year period. Thus, the overall spending stimulus from the war on terror will likely be similar to the extra 2 percent of GDP that was expended at the peak of the Vietnam War. Using the kind of economic response mentioned before, where GDP rose by 60 to 70 cents for each dollar of military outlays, this stimulus is likely to prevent the continuation of the recession into 2002.

One specific favorable effect from the war on terror is that it breaks the nonsensical constraint that the U.S.

Congress had adopted of not invading the social security surplus. The surplus, which had been projected
under one definition of social security to be roughly
$160 billion for 2001, corresponds to payroll taxes (con-
tributions from workers and employers) plus interest
earnings on the social security trust fund less benefit
payments. From the definition, it is obvious that the
social security surplus is independent of spending and
taxing decisions taken by the rest of the government.
Therefore, it is unclear in what sense the remainder of
the federal surplus or deficit would invade or reinforce
the social security surplus, which is the amount that
feeds into the trust fund. Hence, the constraint of keep-
ing the rest of the federal budget surplus above zero so
that the total would remain above $160 billion never
made sense. However, the constraint was not a problem
until the economic boom turned into a slowdown and,
even more so, when the new kind of terrorism brought
us into a war.

Most economists, whether Keynesians or not, agree
that government budget deficits should be large during
temporary economic difficulties, of which the two most
prominent examples are recessions and wars. Recessions
are bad times to collect lots of taxes, and wars are times
in which spending is sharply above normal. In late 2001,
we had both a recession and a war, and it made perfect
sense to have a federal deficit.

Another way in which the September 11 attacks eliminated harmful constraints is that it freed the government

politically to approach international terrorism as the war that it is. Probably this freedom will be the most important long-term consequence from the attacks on New York and Washington.

The extra federal spending for the war on terror will tend to crowd out other candidates for new federal spending, such as education, prescription drug benefits, and an array of social programs. Since I always regarded these programs as mistakes, I regard the pressure to curtail them as a plus.

Not all aspects of wars are favorable for economic activity. For example, the perceived increased risk of flying lowers the demand for air travel, and the perceived higher risk of terrorism likely reduces business investment. However, negative effects were also present in previous wars, including worries about Japanese invasion of the U.S. mainland during World War II and about Soviet missiles during the cold war. Nevertheless, the net effects of previous wars on U.S. GDP turned out to be positive.

The September 11 attacks have also given us a new perspective on airline security, which previously had been mainly the responsibility of the individual airlines. It seems reasonable to regard security in airports and on airplanes as public goods that should be supervised and, perhaps, partly financed by the federal government. The private benefits that the airlines attached to airport and airplane security were clearly much less than the total benefits. Or, to put it another way, the airlines did not bear anything close to the total costs of the terror of

September 11. Hence, airlines as private businesses would, if unregulated, tend to invest too little in security. The low caliber of the typical airport security screener was one manifestation of this situation.

The question of whether airport security personnel should be government or private employees is a more difficult issue. In fact, it is pretty much the same question as whether air traffic controllers should be public or private workers. Experiences in other countries have shown that air traffic control and airport security can work effectively if the employees are private but are subject to appropriate governmental supervision and incentives. On the other hand, we probably do not want to change all police and military personnel into private employees who are publicly supervised. So, the exact place to draw the line is not clear. (However, I feel comfortable in arguing that no postal workers should be federal employees.)

One concern about the situation in late 2001 is all the nonsensical proposals in Washington for fiscal stimulus beyond the expenditures for national security and reconstruction of New York. Whatever is decided about airport and airline security, there is no economic rationale for general bailouts or subsidies of airlines, insurance companies, the steel industry, agriculture, and so on. After all, it is not only during tranquil times that we ought to rely on free markets, rather than the government, to allocate resources. If the risky new world means that air travel is less safe or that threats of domestic terrorism are greater, then the unfettered market will generate less air travel and higher insurance rates. This may also mean fewer functioning airlines and some reorganizations of ownership. These seem to be the correct outcomes at least until our government succeeds at lowering the various threats.

There was also a question in early 2002 about what to do on the tax side of the fiscal equation, specifically, on whether further tax cuts ought to be part of a fiscal stimulus package. One thing the economy surely did not need is more tax rebates, which were probably never a net economic stimulus (as I argued in the previous essay). Accelerating the tax rate cuts that were enacted on a phased-in basis earlier in 2001 would be a good idea. This acceleration would eliminate the contractionary incentives that apply when households and businesses expect future tax rates to be lower than current rates (see, again, the previous essay). Any further changes in tax policy in 2002 would best be targeted at improving incentives for households and businesses to produce and invest. Unfortunately, the effective loss of at least part of the peace dividend from the end of the cold war may mean that some kinds of taxes will have to rise.

Overall, my prediction at the end of 2001 was that the U.S. economy would expand during 2002. However, it was surely possible that the government would come up with a fiscal package that was bad enough to prolong the economic slowdown.

Fiscal Profligacy at the American Economic Association

I have already mentioned how excess funds, caused by a budget surplus, tend to make the U.S. government less disciplined in its spending decisions. My sense is that this tendency to spend "free cash" applies to almost all groups. One might have thought that economists would be different, but the following stories suggest the contrary.

Many years ago, while president of the American Economic Association (AEA), Milton Friedman worried about how to deal with the association's large accumulated surplus. Friedman's view was that an association with lots of money was dangerous because the money would likely be spent on someone's concept of a "socially worthwhile purpose." Friedman solved the problem by providing the membership with an expensive new journal, with no balancing increase in dues. Hence, he eliminated the cumulated surplus by raising spending in a relatively harmless manner. (Dues did rise later to match the increased spending.)

The problem Friedman recognized recurred in 1999. Mostly because of the exuberance of the stock market, the AEA had amassed assets of over $8 million, compared with annual spending of about $4 million. Historically, the association had regarded a reserve of one year's expenses as prudent. Hence, roughly $4 million of the

1999 endowment constituted excess funds. My worry at the time, similar to Friedman's from long before, was that the money would be spent on someone's vision of a socially desirable activity.

My preference was for the excess assets to be returned to the membership through some kind of tax cut. At the time, I was a vice president of the association. In this capacity, I proposed at the January 2, 1999, meeting of the executive committee that the dues be cut in half until the level of assets at the beginning of a calendar year was close to 100 percent of the budgeted expenditures for the coming year. The spirit of this proposal was that a windfall of funds did not provide good reason for new spending programs. Rather, the extra money ought to be given back to the owners.

It was clear during the meeting that this tax-cutting proposal was in trouble. Many committee members thought that the association was well off financially and could therefore afford new expenditure programs. One person wanted to expand the size of the association's main journal. Another wanted to fund a series of symposia. Other ideas for spending involved research on economic education, an expanded study of the role of women in the economics profession, and the provision of information through the Internet. One observer said that this inclination to spend the excess money on something was reminiscent of the way that corporate managers tended to spend free cash flow.

In the end my proposal went down to a crashing defeat. I have several hypotheses about why this happened:

• Officers, as managers, like the idea of having lots of cash so that they can fund various pet programs without much financial restraint.

• The broad interest of the members in tax cuts does not translate into much self-interest of the officers in effecting these cuts. Partly this is because the officers have short terms and do not run for reelection. (For instance, my tenure as vice president was for only one year.)

• Some of the officers liked the notion of using the windfall to effect tax cuts but wanted these cuts to be small and extended over many years. This idea has merit, but it works only if future officers are not tempted to raise spending when they have lots of money available. The same idea applies to the accumulation of a large fund for social security. This idea is attractive only if the government does not react to the existence of the fund by increasing social security benefits.

• Some officers thought that the association's world had become more uncertain especially because of the growth of electronic publishing, so that the prudent level of reserves had risen. This idea may also have merit, but it again works only if future officers do not spend the reserves.

My own inclination is toward the first hypothesis. Basically, the society of economists acted pretty much the same as the U.S. Congress in focusing on current and future ways to spend a windfall of cash. For me, this is a cause of despair. After all, if one cannot trust a group of economists for fiscal restraint, then whom can one trust?

It's the Economy—Economic Evaluations of the U.S. Presidents

When it comes to honesty and (alleged) criminal behavior, the differences between Presidents Nixon and Clinton are arguable. But for economic outcomes, the distinction could not be clearer. Nixon's ouster in 1974 came during the next-to-worst economic record of the thirteen full administrations since the end of World War II. Only the Carter presidency had poorer outcomes. In contrast, Clinton's second term had the best record, except for President Reagan's first term.

The table shows the economic outcomes for the thirteen administrations. The results are summarized by an expanded misery index, a term coined in the 1960s by Lyndon Johnson's economic adviser, Arthur Okun. According to my definition, misery increased if the inflation rate rose, if the unemployment rate went up, if long-term interest rates (a good measure of expected future inflation) increased, and if the growth rate of real gross domestic product (GDP) was below average. The penultimate column sums these items to compute the overall contribution to misery. The last column ranks the administrations, where 1 is best (least added misery) and 13 is worst.

The misery index for the U.S. presidents

President and years	Change in inflation rate	Change in unemploy- ment rate	Change in long-term interest rate	Shortfall of GDP growth	Change in misery index	Rank (1 is best)
Truman II 1949–1952	1.2	0.4	0.3	−2.7	−0.8	6
Eisenhower I 1953–1956	0.2	1.6	0.6	0.7	3.1	11
Eisenhower II 1957–1960	−1.2	1.3	0.5	1.3	1.9	10
Kennedy-Johnson 1961–1964	−0.4	−0.8	0.3	−1.6	−2.5	4
Johnson II 1965–1968	2.2	−1.1	1.5	−1.3	1.3	8
Nixon I 1969–1972	−0.1	1.6	0.0	0.1	1.6	9
Nixon-Ford 1973–1976	4.4	1.5	0.8	1.3	8.0	12
Carter 1977–1980	4.8	−1.3	5.5	0.4	9.4	13
Reagan I 1981–1984	−6.3	1.4	−0.7	0.7	−4.9	1
Reagan II 1985–1988	0.0	−0.8	−2.1	−0.2	−3.1	3
Bush 1989–1992	−0.3	0.9	−1.8	1.7	0.5	7
Clinton I 1993–1996	−0.4	−1.4	−0.8	0.2	−2.4	5
Clinton II 1997–2000	−1.0	−1.0	−1.0	−1.1	−4.1	2

Notes: The change in the consumer price index inflation rate is the difference between the average for the term and the average of the last year of the previous term. The change in the unemployment rate is the difference between the average value during the term and the value from the last month of the previous term. The change in the interest rate is the change in a measure of the long-term government bond yield during the term. (For the last administration, the data are for U.S. Treasury bonds of twenty-year maturity. Earlier figures are for an average of long-term yields.) The GDP growth rate is the shortfall of the rate during the term from 3.1 percent per year (the long-term average value). The change in the misery index is the sum of the first four columns. The rank in the last column goes from lowest to highest misery.

The first Reagan term ranks highly mainly because it broke the back of the inflation that had built up since the late 1960s. The second term featured lower interest rates, which reflected increasing confidence that inflation had been tamed, and good results on economic growth and unemployment. Nowadays, commentators remember mostly the budget deficits. However, as I have already argued, the main consequence of these deficits was the brake on federal spending during the Bush and Clinton administrations.

Clinton followed the mediocre performance of the first Bush presidency with a strong first term. Declines in unemployment, interest rates, and inflation combined with roughly average economic growth to generate a fifth-place ranking, close to the Kennedy-Johnson term.

The second Clinton term brought even better results. The average growth rate of GDP, 4.2 percent, was the best since the Johnson administration, the unemployment rate of 4.0 percent at the end of 2000 was the lowest since 1970, the average CPI inflation rate of 2.3 percent was the lowest since the mid-1980s, and the long-term interest rate of 5.6 percent at the end of 2000 was the lowest since 1968.

The irony is that the same methodology that gives Clinton such high marks places Reagan's first term at the top. No doubt, some partisan observers will argue that my scoring is accurate for Clinton but wrong for Reagan. But a nonpartisan view would accept both verdicts.

It would be nice to know which policies or luck caused Clinton or the other presidents to do as well as they did.

Positive elements for Clinton include trade promotion, welfare reform, reasonable restraint on federal spending, and stable monetary policy. Negative factors, such as the income tax rate hike, minimum wage increase, and overzealous antitrust enforcement, were not large enough to hold back the economy. But the key matter is the absence of a really big domestic policy error, such as Nixon's price controls, Bush's Americans with Disabilities Act, and Clinton's fortunately defeated health care proposal. No doubt, Clinton was also very lucky, at least with respect to economic matters.

As to the younger Bush's presidency, it is too early at the time of this writing to gauge the overall economic performance. However, the luck during 2001 was pretty bad with respect to economic matters. First, there was an economic slowdown that began in late 2000 but will, no doubt, eventually be attributed to Bush. Then came the events of September 11, which exacerbated the slowdown, at least in the short run. But in the longer run, these events may not be contractionary, and the younger Bush may do better economically than his father.

Serious and Nonserious Fiscal Reforms

Since the 1980s, the key question about the U.S. budget deficit has not been whether it would be eliminated—as it was in the second half of the 1990s—but, rather, whether the cuts would feature reductions in spending or increases in tax revenues. The answer during the first half of the 1990s was some of each. In particular, we had the Bush tax increase in 1990 and the Clinton tax increase in 1993. Later, when robust growth produced soaring federal revenues and, hence, budget surpluses, the big question became whether these would be spent or given back to the taxpayers.

The idea that the form of a fiscal adjustment matters more than the amount is the theme of a 1996 study at the International Monetary Fund by Alberto Alesina and Roberto Perotti.[4] They examined the experience with budget deficit reduction in twenty major developed countries in the OECD (Organization for Economic Cooperation and Development) countries from 1960 to 1994.

In 62 of their 378 annual observations, the government was conducting a fiscal adjustment, defined as a reduction in the cyclically adjusted budget deficit by at least 1.5 percent of GDP. However, only about one-quarter of these adjustments were successful three years later, when success is defined to mean that the fall in the fiscal deficit was sustained or that the cumulated reduction in the ratio of the public debt to GDP was by at least five percentage points. Examples of successes were Ireland and Sweden in the late 1980s and Denmark in the mid-1980s. The United States makes the success list only for 1976.

---

4. Alberto Alesina and Roberto Perotti, "Fiscal Adjustment in OECD Countries: Composition and Macroeconomic Effects" (*IMF Staff Papers*, 44, June 1997, 297–329).

The interesting finding in the Alesina-Perotti study is the dependence of a plan's success or failure on the composition of the reform. For one thing, the successful cases concentrated much more on spending reductions than on revenue increases. In the successes, 73 percent of the deficit reduction involved less spending, whereas for the failures, only 44 percent took this form.

The composition of the spending cuts also differed markedly. In the successes, 51 percent of the spending decreases were in transfers and government wages, while 20 percent was in public investment. For the failures, only 17 percent of the reduced spending was on transfers and government wages, whereas a striking 63 percent was in public investment. Referring to the successful reform model as type 1, the authors say, "Type 1 adjustments are most permanent because they tackle the two items of the budget, government wages and welfare programs, which have the strongest tendency to automatically increase."[5] In contrast, in the typical unsuccessful effort, described as type 2, the focus on cuts in public investment reveals a short-run outlook with no lasting commitment to fiscal discipline.

On the revenue side, successful fiscal adjustments focused 62 percent on greater business taxes, whereas only 10 percent was on household taxes and social security contributions. In the unsuccessful cases, 48 percent of the extra revenue came from household taxes and social

5. Ibid., p. 212.

security contributions, while only 21 percent derived from business taxes. Thus, a concentration on household levies is another sign of a type 2, uncommitted reform.

Successful fiscal adjustments are valuable not only because they last but also because they are more favorable for the economy. Economic growth was more rapid under type 1, successful reforms, and this growth was accompanied especially by more robust investment and exports. The authors attribute much of the better economic performance to the enhanced credibility of governments that are willing to undertake sustained reforms: "Governments that are willing to tackle the politically more delicate components of budgets, such as public employment, social security, and welfare programs, may signal that they are really 'serious' about the fiscal adjustment."[6]

Alesina and Perotti go on to describe Italy as a prototypical nonserious country because of its ongoing type 2 fiscal policy. Reductions of fiscal deficits have occurred in Italy from time to time, but the focus has been on more revenue, rather than less spending, and the spending cuts have emphasized public investment.

From the perspective of the Alesina-Perotti study, the method for ending U.S. budget deficits in the 1990s is something of a concern. After all, the main reason the deficits ended is that the government obtained more tax revenues, although mostly from robust growth rather

6. Ibid., p. 217.

than from higher tax rates, not that it curbed spending. Therefore, we ought to be concerned about the permanence of the budget surplus. Things would look more promising if the federal government had followed through on efforts to reduce programs such as Medicare and education rather than shifting to expansions of these programs.

Mr. Greenspan and U.S. Monetary Policy

Some years ago, I wrote a column for *The Wall Street Journal* in which I praised Alan Greenspan, the chairman of the Federal Reserve System, for his committed pursuit of price stability. I happened to see Greenspan the next day at a conference in Jackson Hole, Wyoming, and he went out of his way to commend me for my insightful analysis. Since that time, I have mixed my praise for Greenspan with criticism, especially when he departs from a focus on low inflation to worry about things like the exuberance of stock markets. My feeling is that he regards my subsequent commentaries as somewhat less insightful than the one that he praised in Jackson Hole.

The watershed for U.S. monetary policy came in the early 1980s when the economy faced double-digit rates of interest and inflation. Fed chairman Paul Volcker, supported by President Ronald Reagan, committed monetary policy to conquering this inflation. Even in the face of the 1982 recession, Volcker and Reagan stuck to their guns and managed to establish a credible policy of low inflation.

By the time Greenspan assumed the Fed chairmanship in 1987, the U.S. economy had been performing well for several years. Economic growth was strong, and interest and inflation rates had been much reduced. Hence, Greenspan's task was easier than that of his predecessor. He mainly had to maintain the low-inflation reputation that Volcker had established. Nevertheless, Greenspan deserves credit for carrying out this mission successfully.

A remarkable thing about the Greenspan era is the regular way in which the Fed has managed the Federal Funds rate, which is the interbank interest rate that the Fed controls closely. The rate reacts regularly to a number of economic variables, including inflation and measures of aggregate economic activity. This kind of "reaction function" is often called a Taylor rule, in honor of John Taylor, the Stanford economics professor who enunciated the idea in 1993. Since then (and also earlier because the idea of a Taylor rule preceded Taylor's analysis),[7] numerous researchers have studied these rules. These studies make it possible to build a simple model to explain and forecast the Fed's actions. I have constructed such a model, using data from August 1987 to the present.

---

7. This situation seems to be an example of Stigler's Law, whereby nothing is named after the person who actually invented it. As George Stigler pointed out, this regularity also applies to Stigler's Law.

One unsurprising result is that the Federal Funds rate reacts positively to past inflation, which I measure by the deflator for the gross domestic product. Given this overall measure of inflation, other indicators, such as changes in consumer and producer price indexes (CPI and PPI) or the growth of wages, do not help to predict the Fed's actions. This pattern is surprising for the CPI, because this variable does help to predict inflation calculated from the gross domestic product (GDP) deflator (which is available only quarterly). Since the other inflation variables fail to predict overall inflation, it is not surprising that the Fed does not react to them.

Interest rates tend to rise in response to strong employment growth, which is one indicator of a tight labor market. This reaction seems reasonable because for a given history of inflation, a higher rate of employment growth predicts a higher rate of future inflation. However, there is no indication that "new-economy" effects have changed the nature of this response. Interest rates tend also to rise when the unemployment rate falls, a pattern that is surprising because the unemployment rate turns out not to be a predictor of inflation.

The Fed seems also to react a little to the stock market, raising rates in response to a boom and lowering them in response to a bust. The reason for this behavior is unclear, because the data show that rises in stock prices do not predict higher inflation.

The data also reveal no systematic response of interest rates to GDP growth or to variations in U.S. dollar exchange rates with other major currencies. The lack of response to these variables seems okay because these variables turn out not to predict inflation.

I have some concern about monetary policy during 2001 because the Fed cut interest rates at a pace that was substantially in excess of that predicted from its behavior since mid-1987. The slowing of the economy, as reflected in reduced employment growth and higher rates of unemployment, would have predicted some reductions in rates. But the Fed's rate cuts, which brought the Federal Funds rate below 2% by the end of 2001, were much more than would have been predicted.

The pattern of accelerated rate cuts is worrisome because it might signal that the Fed has become less committed to maintaining low inflation and more interested in attempting to forestall an economic downturn. Given the great achievement of taming inflation from the mid-1980s through the 1990s, this change in policy is probably a mistake. The successes of the past should not convince the Fed that it can now fine-tune the economy to avoid recessions and still maintain low inflation.

In the 1979 movie *Being There*, Peter Sellers plays Chance, a simple gardener who mainly wants to cultivate bushes and flowers. But people think that he is Chauncey Gardiner, and they take his strange utterances about gardens to be sage metaphors for economic policy. Thus, almost everyone comes to believe that Chance knows best about how the economy works, and the president comes to rely on him for all things economic.

The point, of course, is that Fed chairman Greenspan may have come to resemble Chance the Gardener. No doubt because of the good economic times during most of the 1990s, people came to expect wisdom from Greenspan on all aspects of economic life. Moreover, Greenspan has not been shy to expand his commentary beyond monetary policy to include such matters as stock markets, technological change, social security, and fiscal policy.

Frankly, it would be better if Greenspan remained focused on his central mission of monetary policy. Within that mission, it would be best to stick to the objective of low inflation that has proven so successful since the mid-1980s. The end of a career, which presumably Greenspan was approaching in 2001, is not a good time to try something new, different, and reckless.

And the Winner of the 2000 Presidential Election Was . . .

Economists and political scientists have been using models and statistical methods to try to forecast the outcomes of presidential and other elections. One version of this modeling is presented by Alberto Alesina, John Londregan, and Howard Rosenthal.[8] They show that one can do reasonably well for U.S. presidential races by knowing the rate of economic growth during the election

8. Alberto Alesina, John Londregan, and Howard Rosenthal, "The 1992, 1994, and 1996 Elections: A Comment and a Forecast," *Public Choice* 88, 1996, 115–125.

year and the share of the incumbent presidential party's vote in the previous election for members of the House of Representatives. Each additional percentage point of growth raises the projected vote share of the incumbent party in the presidential election by a little more than a percentage point. Each extra percentage point of the incumbent party's share in the previous House vote increases the projected presidential vote share by a little less than a percentage point. In addition, the model implies that the incumbent presidential party has an advantage in the election.

The table shows how this simple model would have done in predicting the outcomes of the previous twenty-two presidential races. The results are expressed in terms of the share of the incumbent party in the votes garnered by the top two candidates; for example, Al Gore and the Democrats received 50.3 percent of this total in 2000. (The model is not set up to deal with third-party candidates. However, since 1916 and except for the 2000 election, the person who received more than 50 percent of the votes cast for the top two contenders has always become president.)

The model has a lot of explanatory power but is surely not perfect. Notable misses of the past are the forecast that Dewey would beat Truman in 1948 with 52 percent of the vote and that Ford would beat Carter in 1976 with 53 percent of the vote. The largest error in terms of vote count is for Johnson in the 1964 election; the model says that he would beat Goldwater with 53 percent of the vote, compared with the actual landslide figure of 61 percent.

Predicted vote for incumbent party in presidential elections

Year (%)	Incumbent party	Actual vote (%)	Predicted vote (%)	Error
1916	Democrat	51.6	53.8	−2.2
1920	Democrat	36.2	39.2	−3.0
1924	Republican	65.3	60.5	4.8
1928	Republican	58.8	62.1	−3.3
1932	Republican	40.8	39.3	1.5
1936	Democrat	62.5	65.8	−3.3
1940	Democrat	55.0	54.5	0.4
1944	Democrat	53.8	52.4	1.3
1948	Democrat	52.3	45.6	6.7
1952	Democrat	44.6	49.3	−4.7
1956	Republican	57.7	54.4	3.3
1960	Republican	49.9	51.7	−1.8
1964	Democrat	61.3	52.8	8.6
1968	Democrat	49.6	50.6	−1.0
1972	Republican	61.8	56.7	5.1
1976	Republican	48.9	53.2	−4.2
1980	Democrat	44.7	47.7	−3.0
1984	Republican	59.2	57.3	1.9
1988	Republican	53.9	54.8	−0.9
1992	Republican	46.5	52.8	−6.3
1996	Democrat	54.7	47.1	7.6
2000	Democrat	50.3	48.7	1.6

Note: The vote percentage refers to the share of the incumbent party in the total votes cast for the two top parties. The predicted value comes from the model described in the text. The error is the shortfall in percentage points of the incumbent party's vote share from its predicted value.

The two Clinton races also show up as errors. The model predicted that he would lose with 47 percent of the vote in 1992 and 1996; instead, he got 53 percent in the first race and 55% in the second. The elder Bush was supposed to win in 1992 because he was the incumbent and because the economy grew at the reasonable rate of 2.3 percent in 1992. Clinton was supposed to lose in 1996 mostly because the Democratic party's share of the House vote in 1994 was only 47 percent. This consideration was only partly offset in the model by the strong economic growth of 3.8 percent in 1996.

Despite the misses of the 1990s, the longer-term good performance of the model might make us interested in the results for 2000. One consideration is that the share of the Democrats in the House vote for 1998 was nearly 50 percent (much better than in 1994). With the economy growing at a rate of 3.4 percent rate for 2000, the projected vote share for the Democratic presidential candidate in 2000 was 48.7 percent. Given the margins of error in the statistical estimate, this result should be read as saying that the 2000 election was too close to call. In this sense, the model accorded well with the actual outcome, which was essentially an even split between the Democrats and the Republicans.

Oil—The Good Guys and the Bad Guys

"Our friends came through for us," U.S. Energy Secretary Bill Richardson said in 2000 after a run-up in oil prices. He was referring to a period of increases in oil production by Saudi Arabia, Kuwait, the United Arab Emirates, and Mexico. Indeed, oil prices did fall from $32 per barrel in March 2000 (for West Texas intermediate crude) to about $25 later in the year. But one has to wonder why our "friends" were in a position to raise oil production so quickly. Perhaps they had been holding down production and were thereby partly responsible for the rise in oil prices from around $12 per barrel in early 1999.

This view is confirmed by the table, which gives numbers on output and capacity in March 2001 for the main oil producers. (Capacity is an estimate of the oil that a country can produce quickly without a significant rise in recovery costs per barrel.) The last column shows the percentage of utilized capacity. The main excess capacity early in 2001 was in Saudi Arabia and Kuwait, two countries that Richardson regarded as friends.

Although the United States was roughly comparable to Saudi Arabia as a producer of oil—around 8 million barrels per day—the U.S. consumption of nearly 20 million barrels made it the largest net importer of oil. Therefore, the United States as a whole benefits from lower oil prices. In fact, the rises in oil prices up to the early 1980s, and perhaps in 1990, were substantial contributors to U.S. recessions. From this perspective, the good guys among the oil producers are the ones who produce as much as possible. Thus, within the Organization of Petroleum Exporting Countries (OPEC), the relatively "friendly" countries include Iran, Venezuela, Iraq (when it is allowed by the West to produce oil), Nigeria (whose

Oil production and capacity, March 2001

Country	Production	Capacity	Percentage of capacity used
	(millions of barrels per day)		
Major OPEC			
Saudi Arabia	8.0	10.5	76
Iran	3.8	3.9	97
Venezuela	3.0	3.0	100
Iraq	2.8	2.8	96
Kuwait	1.8	2.5	72
United Arab Emirates	2.3	2.5	92
Nigeria	2.1	2.2	95
Libya	1.4	1.4	100
Indonesia	1.2	1.2	100
Other largest			
United States	8.3	8.3	100
Former U.S.S.R.	8.2	8.2	100
Mexico	3.6	3.6	100
Norway	3.4	3.4	100
China	3.2	3.2	100
Canada	2.8	2.8	100
United Kingdom	2.6	2.6	100
Brazil	1.6	1.6	100

Source: International Energy Agency, *Oil Market Report* (April 2001). Data for OPEC countries include crude oil only and are therefore understated by about 10 percent relative to those for the other countries. Capacity numbers for non-OPEC countries assume (apparently realistically) zero excess capacity.

capacity has been reduced by civil unrest), and Libya. The bad guys are those who hold down production in relation to capacity. Hence, the main culprits early in 2001 were our supposed friends, Saudi Arabia and Kuwait. Earlier, Mexico was also somewhat unfriendly, because it became in 1998 the only non-OPEC country to maintain significant spare capacity. We also ought not to ascribe all increases in oil production to friendship. A pure profit motive would explain why these countries increased production when oil prices were high.

Richardson also said that the oil prices of around $12 per barrel in early 1999 were too low, the peak prices of around $32 in March 2000 were too high, and the subsequent prices of around $25 were about right. One wonders how he knew all this. Does he also know the just prices of wheat, copper, gold, and shares of Microsoft? Probably he meant that his friends in the U.S. oil business and the Middle East were unhappy when the price was $12 and that $32—while even better from the producers' perspective—did not seem to be sustainable in the world market. (However, Richardson's analysis may have been keener than I thought, because shortly after he left the government, he was rewarded with a position as lecturer at Harvard's Kennedy School of Government.)

As for most goods, there is a lot to say for letting the market figure out the right price of oil. Admittedly, there may be a valid national security argument for maintaining more U.S. domestic oil production than would result at the free market price, whether that turned out to be $12 or $32. But, then, the best first step to ensure adequate domestic supplies would be to reduce the restrictive policies that hinder exploration and production. For example, we could, as the Bush administration was arguing in 2002, expand the development of oil in Alaska and off-shore sites.

A bad policy is to support the world oil cartel in its attempts to maintain artificially high prices for oil. It is particularly odd when a U.S. government official labels as friends foreign governments that are carrying out acts—collusive behavior to fix prices—that would be regarded as criminal if done within the United States. Perhaps it would be better if U.S. oil policy were run out of the Justice Department rather than the Energy Department.

Exuberance and Pessimism in the U.S. Stock Market

In the middle of 2000, when the stock market had been booming, a key question was whether the market was too high or too low. One view was that the market, especially the Nasdaq with its emphasis on technology stocks, was overpriced and would eventually come down. The overpricing of stocks might reflect *Irrational Exuberance*, the title of a book by Robert Shiller.[9] This view turned out to look good after the fact.

---

9. Robert Shiller, *Irrational Exuberance* (Princeton, N.J.: Princeton University Press, 2000).

The second idea was that the market was underpriced and would eventually go up a lot more, as argued in *Dow 36,000* by James Glassman and Kevin Hassett.[10] The alleged causes of the underpricing include exaggeration of risks and underestimation of growth prospects.

The last possibility is that the market was pricing prospective earnings efficiently in a complex environment. Fed chairman Greenspan eventually came around to this view, although he earlier expressed concerns about irrational exuberance. (Greenspan apparently coined this phrase but may have gotten the idea from a presentation by Shiller at the Federal Reserve Board.)

The competing theories can be examined with a formula for the price-earnings (P/E) ratio, one of the favorite measures of stock valuation. Abstracting from taxes on dividends and capital gains, the formula is

$$P/E = 1/(r-g).$$

The variable r is the expected real rate of return required by holders of stock; it equals the risk-free rate plus a risk premium. The variable g is the prospective, hypothetical growth rate of real dividends per share that would arise if no earnings were retained by corporations. P/E is the ratio of price per share to earnings per share.

We can apply the formula by using numbers from 1871 to 1997 from Jeremy Siegel's book, *Stocks for the Long*

10. James Glassman and Kevin Hassett, *Dow 36,000* (New York: Times Business/Random House, 1999).

Run.[11] The average real rate of return on U.S. stocks was 7.0 percent per year, which gives an historical measure of *r*. The variable *g* is harder to quantify, but it should be less than the growth rate of real dividends per share, which was 1.2 percent per year. If we use 1.0 percent for *g*, then the formula gives a P/E ratio of 16.7, which is close to the historical median of 14.

Siegel notes that the average real rate of return on short-term government securities was 1.7 percent per year, which provides an estimate of the average risk-free rate. (Risk-free rates in 2000 were around 4 percent, based on the yields on inflation-indexed U.S. Treasury bonds and therefore exceeded the historical average.) Hence, the 7.0% real return on stocks implies that the risk premium averaged 5.3 percent. Economists have long puzzled about why this premium has been so high, and Siegel adds to the puzzle by noting that stocks have actually been less risky than government bonds for holding periods of ten years or more.

The Siegel observation on risk is the main content of the Glassman-Hassett book (which, however, has a much catchier title). They think that the proper risk premium on stocks is close to zero, so that *r* should approximate the risk-free rate, historically around 2 percent and more recently about 4 percent. When combined with a value for *g* of 1 percent, the formula implies P/E ratios between 33 and 100. Hence, this perspective suggested no reason

11. Jeremy Siegel, *Stocks for the Long Run*, 2nd ed. (New York: McGraw-Hill, 1998).

to worry about the observed P/E ratios of around 40 for the S&P 500 stock index in mid-2000. This conclusion is strengthened if one uses new-economy thinking to raise the estimate of g above 1 percent. These kinds of arguments led Glassman and Hassett to predict a boom in stock prices as the market gradually caught on to the "reality" of low risk and high growth prospects. Apparently, however, the collapse of tech stocks starting later in 2000 represented reductions in growth prospects, that is, in g, as well as possible increases in the risk premium on stocks.

Shiller's view is that future values of r and g will likely not differ much, on average, from their historical values. Thus, for him, much of the observed fluctuation in P/E ratios represents excess price volatility. Notably, the high ratio in mid-2000 reflected irrational exuberance in the forms of overstated growth prospects and understated risk premia. He predicted that the bubble would eventually burst, and the P/E ratio would come crashing down to normal.

Greenspan's view (revised from earlier) is apparently that growth prospects and the riskiness of stock returns are hard to pin down when new technologies are having a large and uncertain impact on productivity. Thus, changing views can create substantial volatility of P/E ratios, especially on the tech-heavy Nasdaq market. At any point in time, the market price represents a reasonable aggregation of the various beliefs, including, in 2000, those like Shiller's that predicted a crash and those like

Glassman and Hassett's that expected a boom. There is no reason to think that the resulting price at any moment is systematically too high or too low. My view is that this position is the most reasonable one to take when assessing the stock market. Although Shiller happened to be right in 2000, a different viewpoint will probably look brilliant the next time.

This conclusion forces me to remember that I was once interviewed by a major financial firm to see whether I might like to abandon my ivory-tower academic life to become their chief economist. They said, however, that if I worked on Wall Street, I would have to go beyond the position that financial markets were efficient. Since I still work in ivory towers, I can perhaps be forgiven for having just taken this position.

Index